Volume 2
CELL BIOLOGY

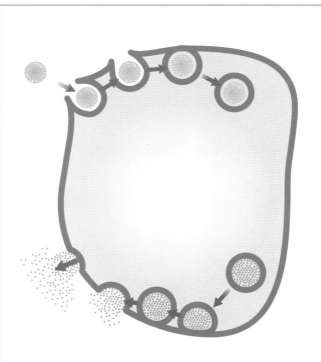

GROLIER

Published 2004 by Grolier
An imprint of Scholastic Library Publishing
Old Sherman Turnpike
Danbury, Connecticut 06816

FOR THE BROWN REFERENCE GROUP plc
Contributors: Derek Harvey, Amy-Jane
                       Beer, Ph.D., Natalie Goldstein
Consultant: Erin Dolan, PhD
                       Virginia Polytechnic Institute
                       and State University
Project Editor: Anne Wanjie
Deputy Editor: Jim Martin
Development Editor: Richard Beatty
Copy Editors: Lesley Campbell-Wright
                       John Jackson
Designer: Joan Curtis
Picture Researcher: Becky Cox
Illustrators: Darren Awuah, Richard Burgess,
                       Mark Walker
Indexer: Kay Ollerenshaw
Managing Editor: Bridget Giles
Design Manager: Lynne Ross
Production Director: Alastair Gourlay
Editorial Director: Lindsey Lowe

Printed and bound in Singapore

ABOUT THIS SET

What could be more fascinating than the story of life? It is all told in *Biology Matters!* Across ten topical volumes this set reviews all fundamental life-science concepts. Each volume carefully introduces its topic, briefly examines the history, and fully displays all aspects of modern thinking about biology, ecology, evolution, genetics, cell biology, microbiology, life forms from every kingdom, and the human body. The clear text explains complex concepts and terms in full. Hundreds of photographs, artworks, and "Closeup" boxes provide details on key aspects. Simple, safe experiments encourage readers to explore biology in "Try This" boxes. "What Do You Think?" panels pose questions that test the reader's comprehension. "Applications" boxes show how biological knowledge enhances daily life and technology, while "Red Herring" boxes outline failed theories. "Hot Debate" panels illuminate the disagreements and discussions that rage in the biological sciences, and "Genetic Perspective" boxes outline the latest genetic research.

Volume ISBN 0-7172-5981-1
Set ISBN 0-7172-5979-X

Library of Congress Cataloging-in-Publication Data

Biology Matters!
    p. cm.
    Contents: v.1. Introduction to biology—v.2. Cell biology—v.3. Genetics—v.4.
Microorganisms—v.5. Plants—v.6. Animals—v.7. The human body—v.8.
Reproduction—v.9. Evolution—v.10. Ecology.
    ISBN 0-7172-5979-X (set : alk.paper)—ISBN 0-7172-5980-3 (v.1 : alk. paper)—
ISBN 0-7172-5981-1 (v.2 : alk. paper)—ISBN 0-7172-5982-X (v.3 : alk. paper)—
ISBN 0-7172-5983-8 (v.4 : alk. paper)—ISBN 0-7172-5984-6 (v.5 : alk. paper)—
ISBN 0-7172-5985-4 (v.6 : alk. paper)—ISBN 0-7172-5986-2 (v.7 : alk. paper)—
ISBN 0-7172-5987-0 (v.8 : alk. paper)—ISBN 0-7172-5988-9 (v.9 : alk. paper)—
ISBN 0-7172-5989-7 (v.10 : alk. paper)
    1. Biology—Juvenile literature. [1. Biology.] I. Grolier Publishing Company

QH309.2.B56 2004
507—dc22
                                                    2003056942

PICTURE CREDITS (b=bottom; t=top)
Front Cover: Corbis: Jim Zukerman.
Biophotos Inc: Kerry Dressler 11; The Brown
Reference Group plc: 42t, 42b, 48; Corbis: Lester V.
Bergman 5, 6, 7, 12, 13, 16, 32, 69, Ron Boardman 15,
Ron Boardman; Frank Lane Picture Agency 29, Boston
Herald/Wilco/Corbis Sygma 61, Cloud Hill Imaging
Ltd 18, 38, 40t, 40b, Mark Gamba 43, Lynn Goldsmith
50, Bob Krist 4, Douglas P. Wilson; Frank Lane Picture
Agency 53, Jim Zukerman 10; Imagingbody.com: 31;
Photos.com: 52; Rex Features: Gustafsson 44, Phanie
Agency 56; Science Photo Library: Deep Light
Productions 70, Manfred Kage 20, Professors P. Motta
& T. Naguro 41, Dr Howard Smedley 62; Topham:
65, Chris Fitzgerald/Imageworks 54.

CONTENTS

Volume 2
Cell Biology

What Is a Cell?	4
Types of Cells	10
Movement and Support	20
Inside the Cell	30
Cell Communication	44
The Cell Cycle	52
Cells Out of Control	62
Glossary	71
More Information	73
Set Index	74

1 What Is a Cell?

▼ *Ostrich eggs contain the largest single cells on Earth. Each cell is the yolk cell that provides food for the growing ostrich chick. However, the yolk cells inside the eggs of many dinosaurs and some giant extinct birds such as moas were probably much larger.*

Cells are the building blocks of life. Your body contains trillions of cells, but many creatures are just a single cell.

Many areas of biology depend on an understanding of cells. The largest single cell, an ostrich egg yolk, is the size of a baseball, but cells can be so tiny that a hundred placed in a row would fit on the period at the end of this sentence. Tiny cells such as protists (see **4**: 20–31) and bacteria (see **4**: 8–19) are usually measured in nanometers. A nanometer is 1 millionth of a millimeter. Most plants and animals are made up of billions or even trillions of cells. The study of cells is called cytology.

Cells work together to carry out important functions within an organism. Many cells are specialized to carry out certain tasks. Red blood cells, for example, are specialized for transporting oxygen around the body (see 59–60).

Organisms like bacteria consist of just single cells. Each cell carries out all the processes it needs to survive.

The life of a cell

The cells that make up your body go through a life cycle (see 52–61). It consists of a period of growth followed by division to produce a new pair of cells. During the period

▼ *A slice of cork under a light microscope. Robert Hooke would have seen something similar as he peered through his microscope in 1667.*

SEEING CELLS

The first microscope was made by a Dutch eyeglass-maker, Zacharias Janssen (1580–*c.*1638). Later scientists improved on this early version. Englishman Robert Hooke (1635–1703) used his microscope to look closely at a thin slice of cork. Hooke used the word *cell* to describe the units he could see, since they reminded him of the small rooms called cells that monks lived in.

Hooke believed the cork cells were empty and that the walls were made of living material. Improvements in microscope design enabled Dutch scientist Anton van Leeuwenhoek (1632–1723) to study the cellular world in far greater detail. Leeuwenhoek was the first person to see protists, blood cells, and sperm. He also noted the presence of some cell contents such as the chloroplasts, though he was unable to describe them accurately.

In the nineteenth century microscope technology advanced further. Cytologists (cell biologists) could fully observe cells and their contents. Study of the very finest detail became possible with the invention of the electron microscope in the 1950s (see **1**: 50–51).

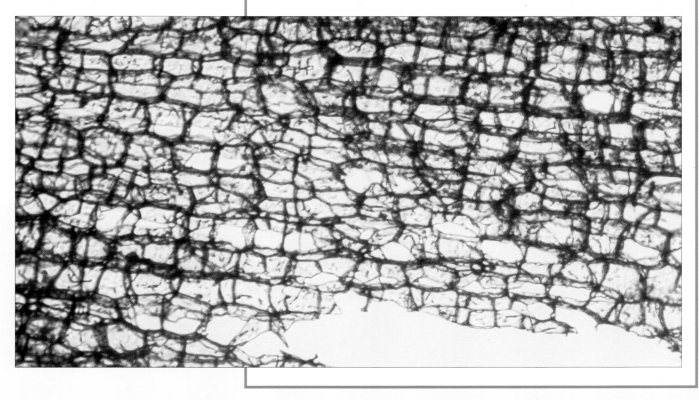

THE CELL THEORY

Although cells were discovered and named by Robert Hooke, the idea that cells form the basic unit of living organisms was established by German biologists Matthias Schleiden (1804–1881) and Theodor Schwann (1810–1882). This became known as the cell theory. Schleiden studied plant cells, and Schwann studied animal cells. Later, German physician Rudolf Virchow (1821–1902) showed that all cells arise from preexisting cells through cell division (see 52–61).

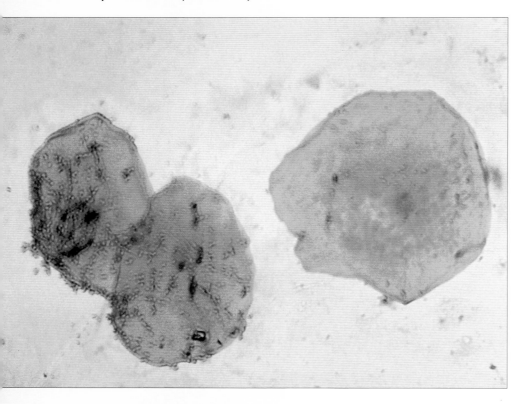

▼ *These are cheek cells. They are easy to collect from the inside of a person's cheek. Cheek cells are often the source of DNA used for DNA fingerprinting, an important tool in police work (see 1: 55).*

of growth cells produce chemicals, make energy from food, and provide structural support for the organism. Communication between the different parts of a cell and between a cell and its neighbors is very important (see 44–51) to ensure they work together for the benefit of the organism.

Cells contain structures such as the cell membrane, cell wall (in plants and bacteria only), and a series of fibers called the cytoskeleton. They support the cell. Movement (see 20–29) often depends on hairlike extensions of the cell. Long single extensions are called flagella. Groups of shorter projections that beat rhythmically are called cilia.

Building systems

Similar cells work together and become specialized in their functions to form tissues, such as muscles or blood in animals (see **1**: 11). A number of tissues working together make up an organ, such as a heart, stomach, or kidney. Groups of organs work together to form systems, such as the digestive system (see **7**: 8–17).

EUKARYOTE EVOLUTION

Scientists believe that the mitochondria that occur inside eukaryote cells descend from free-living prokaryotes. This theory is called endosymbiosis. Evidence comes from the fact that mitochondria have their own DNA separate from the nucleus (see **3**: 48–49).

Around 1.5 billion years ago a prokaryote engulfed the mitochondrion ancestor.

Rather than being digested, the mitochondrion stayed alive, providing energy to the other cell and getting a safe place to live in return. Over millions of years of evolution the two cells became inseparable.

Eukaryotes probably evolved from such a union of cells. Chloroplasts are also thought to be the result of an ancient endosymbiosis.

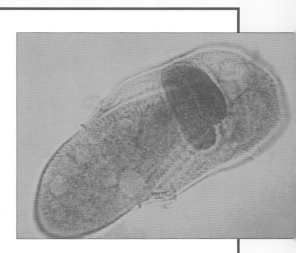

One protist engulfs another. An event like this led to the evolution of eukaryote cells.

Types of cells

Cytologists divide cells into two types, prokaryotes and eukaryotes. Prokaryotes are creatures such as bacteria. They are single-celled organisms, although some occur in chains or clusters of many thousands of individuals.

The DNA of a prokaryote cell floats freely in a region called the nucleoid. The rest of the cell is called the cytoplasm. It contains a thick, jellylike liquid called cytosol and tiny structures called ribosomes. Ribosomes use instructions encoded in the DNA to produce proteins. The cell is wrapped by a cell (plasma) membrane and, in many cases, a tough wall too.

A TYPICAL PROKARYOTE CELL

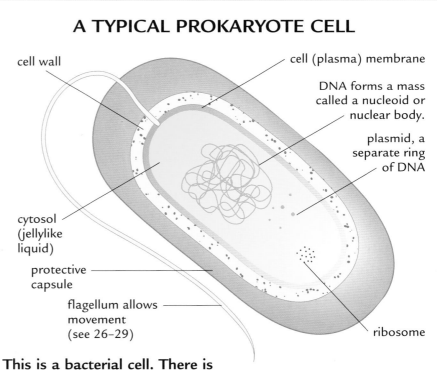

cell wall

cell (plasma) membrane

DNA forms a mass called a nucleoid or nuclear body.

plasmid, a separate ring of DNA

cytosol (jellylike liquid)

protective capsule

flagellum allows movement (see 26–29)

ribosome

This is a bacterial cell. There is great diversity of bacterial form and function, but all have ribosomes, a cell membrane and wall, and DNA loose in a nucleoid, which is not enclosed by a membrane.

TRY THIS

SEEING PLANT CELLS

Take a celery stalk, and put one end in some water with some blue ink or food coloring added. After an hour remove the celery and rinse it. Then cut the stalk into pieces, and examine the cut ends. You will see tiny spots of color. They are sections through bundles of cells that run through the stalk called xylem (see 13). They carry water from the roots to the leaves.

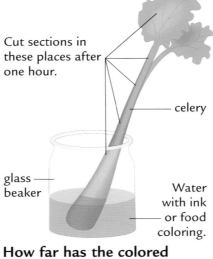

Cut sections in these places after one hour.

celery

glass beaker

Water with ink or food coloring.

How far has the colored water traveled in one hour?

EUKARYOTE CELLS

Like prokaryotes, eukaryote cells have a cytoplasm, cell membrane, and ribosomes.

But they are usually much larger, and they contain many other features absent in prokaryotes. They include a series of fibers called the cytoskeleton (see 24–26). It moves materials around and maintains cell shape. There are also membrane-bound structures called organelles (see 30–43). They do much of the cell's work. The nucleus (see 32–33) is the largest organelle. It contains DNA, which is the cell's genetic (inherited) information (see **3**: 26–37).

Other organelles include the endoplasmic reticulum (see 33–35), which packages proteins; lysosomes (see 37), inside which large molecules

CLOSEUP

WHY ARE CELLS SO SMALL?

As an object gets bigger, its volume increases more quickly than its surface area does. Look how the ratio of surface area to volume drops with size in these cubes. The same thing happens with cells. They need a high surface area-to-volume ratio to work efficiently. That is why most cells are tiny. It also explains why large organisms must be made up of many small cells rather than just a few giant ones.

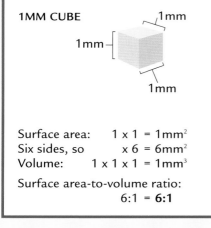

1MM CUBE

1mm

1mm

1mm

Surface area: 1 x 1 = 1mm^2
Six sides, so   x 6 = 6mm^2
Volume: 1 x 1 x 1 = 1mm^3

Surface area-to-volume ratio:
            6:1 = **6:1**

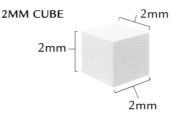

2MM CUBE

2mm

2mm

2mm

Surface area: 2 x 2 = 4mm^2
Six sides, so   x 6 = 24mm^2
Volume: 2 x 2 x 2 = 8mm^3

Surface area-to-volume ratio:
            24:8 = **3:1**

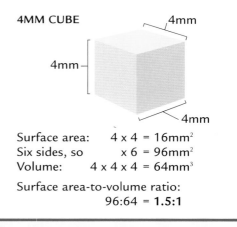

4MM CUBE

4mm

4mm

4mm

Surface area: 4 x 4 = 16mm^2
Six sides, so   x 6 = 96mm^2
Volume: 4 x 4 x 4 = 64mm^3

Surface area-to-volume ratio:
            96:64 = **1.5:1**

are broken down; the mito-chondria (see 40–42), which produce energy from food; and, in plants, algae, and some bacteria, chloroplasts (see 40), which harvest the sun's energy to make food.

Plants, algae, and fungi

Plant and algal cells have strong walls that lie over their cell membranes. Plant cells also contain a large sac called a vacuole, which can make up more than 70 percent of the volume of the cell. The vacuole takes in water and begins to swell. That pushes the cytoplasm against the cell wall, making the cell rigid and giving the plant stability and strength.

The cells of fungi such as mushrooms are similar in some ways to plant cells. They usually contain vacuoles, and their cells have tough walls. However, fungal cells do not have chloroplasts. That is because, like animals, fungi do not photosynthesize. Instead, fungi get the energy they need by breaking down dead and decaying material.

Animal cells

Animal cells are usually smaller than plant cells. The main difference between the structures of animal and plant cells is that animal cells do not have vacuoles or tough cell walls. The membranes of animal cells are made of a flexible material, so the cells can change their shape and size easily. For movement and support animal cells produce bones, cartilage (see 15), or shells and tissues like muscles.

PROTIST DIVERSITY

The most complex single cells belong to the eukaryote group called protists (see **4**: 20–31). Protists are a group of incredible diversity. Some photosynthesize, while others hunt. Protists move in many different ways, but many stay in one place. Protist features include light receptors, sensory bristles, poison darts, leglike body extensions, and even bundles that contract just like muscles.

▶ *This is an animal cell. Plant cells are a little different. They have a tough cell wall and organelles called chloroplasts that trap the energy of sunlight.*

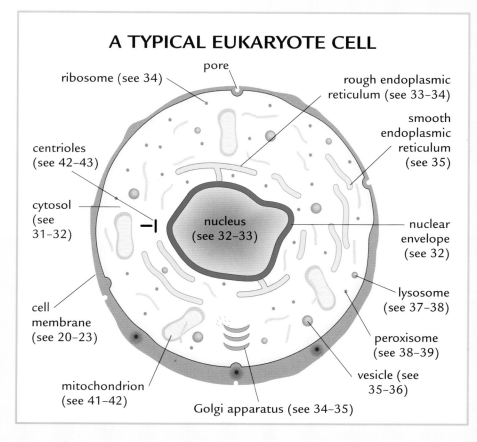

A TYPICAL EUKARYOTE CELL

- ribosome (see 34)
- pore
- rough endoplasmic reticulum (see 33–34)
- smooth endoplasmic reticulum (see 35)
- centrioles (see 42–43)
- cytosol (see 31–32)
- nucleus (see 32–33)
- nuclear envelope (see 32)
- cell membrane (see 20–23)
- lysosome (see 37–38)
- peroxisome (see 38–39)
- vesicle (see 35–36)
- mitochondrion (see 41–42)
- Golgi apparatus (see 34–35)

2 Types of Cells

There is tremendous diversity among the cells that form tissues and organs in organisms.

A plant or animal can be made up of trillions of cells. Different cells carry out different tasks. A tough chemical, cellulose, occurs in plant cell walls, giving them rigidity. By contrast, animal cells are flexible so they can change size and shape.

Groups of cells that work together to carry out certain functions form tissues. Some tissues, such as the pith of plants, are made up of cells of the same type. Other tissues are complex mixtures of many different types of cells. For example, many types of plant cells are required to form structures such as flowers, leaves, and seeds.

Animals contain a range of different types of cells too. Multicellular (many-celled) animals contain structures

▼ *These disk-shaped cells on the inner wall of an artery are red blood cells. Formed in the bone marrow (see 60), red blood cells shuttle oxygen and carbon dioxide around the body. Blood is a type of connective tissue (see 15).*

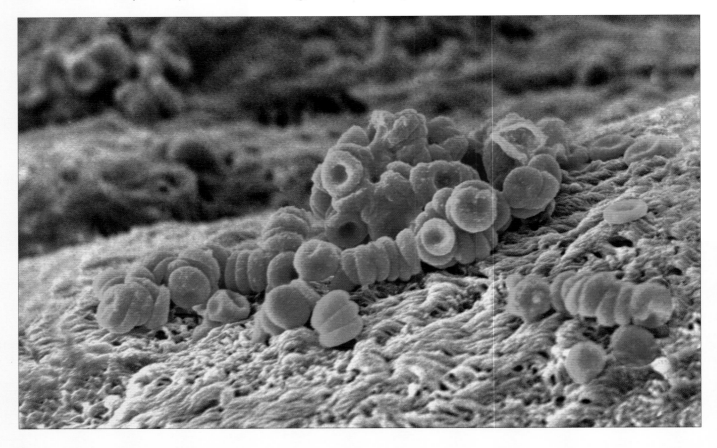

INSIDE SEX CELLS

The sex cells—sperm and eggs—are specialized single cells (see **8**: 18–20). Sperm are tiny. They have a whiplike tail called a flagellum that they use to get around. They have mitochondria for energy, but very little cytoplasm. All a sperm contributes to a zygote (fertilized egg) is its genetic material. Egg cells are much larger. They contain food supplies for the zygote as well as a supply of all the organelles it will need as it develops.

that provide support, such as shells, exoskeletons (see **1**: 36), or bones. Cells forming these structures are called support cells. Organisms also contain lining and nerve cells, and often muscle cells too.

PLANT CELLS

Plant cells are often larger than animal cells. Plant cells contain large water-filled packages called vacuoles. The water inside exerts a force on the membrane enclosing the vacuole. This is called turgor pressure. It causes cells to become turgid (rigid).

Turgid cells tightly packed together produce a very firm type of tissue. It provides the main means of support for plants other than those strengthened by wood. When nonwoody plants are deprived of water for a time, the plant loses turgor pressure. The vacuoles shrink, and the structural tissues lose their firmness. Soon the plant begins to wilt.

▼ *Turgor pressure allows these pitcher plants to stand tall. However, if the rate of water loss through the leaves exceeds the rate of water uptake at the roots, the plants lose turgor pressure. Then they wilt.*

GENETIC SWITCHES

All the cells in an organism result from many divisions of a single fertilized egg cell. With the exception of sex cells (see 60-61), all the cells in an organism are genetically identical. How, then, can they perform different functions?

Different cells use different parts of their genome (genetic instructions). For example, a pancreas cell uses genes that code for digestive juices. Although genes that code for other features, such as bone repair or hair growth, are present, they are not expressed by these cells. The characteristics of a certain cell depend on stretches of DNA called regulator genes. They function as switches and can turn other genes on or off.

▼ *This is a section through a lilac leaf. The horizontal cells at the top are epithelial cells. The vertical cells are parenchyma; they contain chloroplasts.*

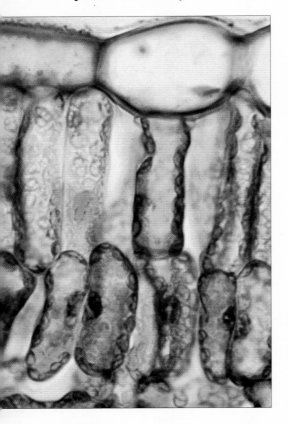

Structural tissues called parenchyma form the bulk of nonwoody plants. Parenchyma cells in the pith, deep inside the plant, are not exposed to light. They are of no use for photosynthesis, the process of making sugars using carbon dioxide gas and sunlight (see **5**: 6–12). So pith parenchyma cells lack chloroplasts, the miniorgans inside which photosynthesis occurs.

Inside the leaf

Chloroplasts do occur in the parenchyma cells of leaves. The outermost layer of the leaf is called the epidermis.

PLANT EPIDERMAL CELLS

Take a look at the leaf surfaces of different plants in your backyard. Many plants show specializations in their epidermis. For example, they might have hairs or spines, or have a thick, waxy outer layer. How do you account for the different shapes and colors of leaves from different plant species?

Thicker leaves have broad parenchyma layers and may also have thick waxy layers. These features might prevent plants from losing too much water in dry environments. Darker leaves may have more chloroplasts. The plant might grow in a shady place, so it needs more chloroplasts to make the most of the reduced light.

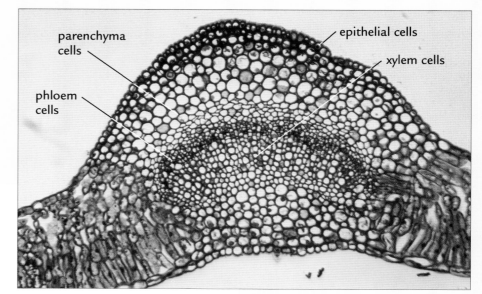

▶ *A section through a leaf rib. Xylem cells are in the center, surrounded by a thin layer of phloem. It is skirted by parenchyma cells, with epithelial cells around the outside.*

Epidermal cells produce a waxy coating on their outer cell walls. It acts as a barrier against water loss, as well as disease organisms and insect enemies. Epidermal cell walls must be thin, though; otherwise not enough light can reach the chloroplasts inside.

Strength and support
Other plant cells have thicker walls. They provide support for the plant. Support cells occur wherever extra strength is needed, in the leaf stalk, for example. Collenchyma cells are stretchy support cells. Their walls become so thick that the cell itself dies. These dead cells form the tough outer layers of the shells of nuts and seeds.

Xylem and phloem cells
The thick-walled cells that strengthen a plant also form long transport vessels. Xylem tissue is formed of hollow, dead cells. Water is drawn

into the plant's roots. It then moves up the xylem to the leaves. There water is lost through a process called transpiration that is caused by water evaporating from pores

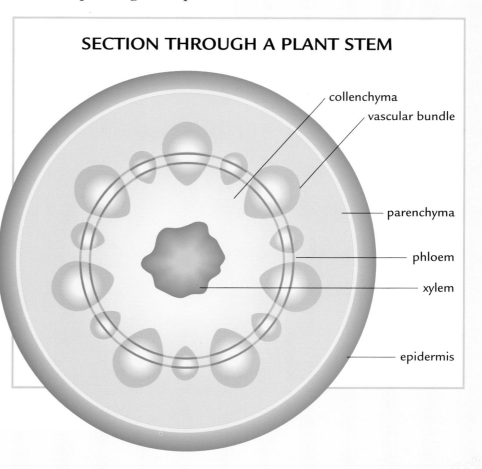

SECTION THROUGH A PLANT STEM

collenchyma
vascular bundle
parenchyma
phloem
xylem
epidermis

in the leaves into the air. Transpiration sucks the water up through the xylem. Xylem also forms wood in trees.

Sugars and other molecules also need to be carried through the plant. Dissolved in water, they move around the plant through a different system of cells called the phloem. Unlike dead xylem cells, phloem cells are alive. A mesh of tiny pores allows the contents of one phloem cell to flow into the next.

ANIMAL CELLS

Scientists divide animal tissues into four main groups depending on the way they develop in the embryo. They are lining, supporting, muscle, and nerve cells.

Lining cells

Epithelial (lining) cells join to form sheets that cover the surface of the body as well as the outer surfaces of organs. The inner surfaces of organs are lined by endothelial cells.

TYPES OF ANIMAL EPITHELIAL CELLS

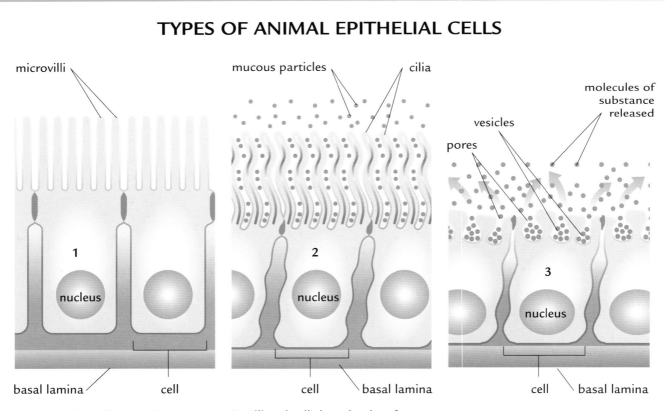

1. Absorptive cells have tiny, fingerlike extensions called microvilli. They increase the area available for absorption of molecules enormously. The walls of the gut are lined by these types of cells.

2. Ciliated cells have banks of tail-like cilia that beat to move things suspended in fluid, such as mucus. Mucus in the windpipe is moved by ciliated cells. Cilia help many tiny organisms get around.

3. Secretory cells contain vesicles (chemical packages). The vesicles rupture to release a substance onto a body surface, such as the skin or into the gut. Sweat glands, for example, are lined by secretory cells.

Cells on the skin's surface divide rapidly to replace cells that are sloughed (brushed off). Epithelial cells that line the air sacs of lungs form a tissue just one cell thick. It allows oxygen to pass easily into the blood and carbon dioxide to move out (see **7**: 26–33). Cells lining the windpipe are shaped like columns. They are covered with tiny projections called cilia (see 27–29). The cilia wave in unison to send mucus to the back of the throat, where it is swallowed.

Cells line small sacs called glands. Glands release products such as hormones (see **7**: 54–55). Glands in the gut release chemicals called enzymes that digest food. Sweat glands are tubes that empty onto the skin. During exercise the glands fill with water and dissolved salts. These constituents of sweat pass into and through epithelial cells lining the sweat glands.

Supporting cells

Tissues important for packing and support are called connective tissues. Cartilage, bone, and blood are all types of connective tissues. Their

▲ *Adipose, or fat, tissue is a type of connective tissue. The liquid-filled cells serve as energy supplies, cushion the internal organs, and insulate the body against the cold.*

CLOSEUP

ERRORS IN DIFFERENTIATION

Sometimes errors occur in cell differentiation. If white blood cells start to multiply uncontrollably, a kind of cancer of the blood called leukemia develops. There are two types of white blood cells, granulocytes and lymphocytes. Similarly there are two types of leukemia. The type of disease depends on which blood cells are multiplying.

INTO THE PAST

CANALS, HEAT, AND DINOSAUR GROWTH

In 1974 French anatomist Armand de Ricqles made an exciting discovery. De Ricqles looked at thin slices of fossilized dinosaur bone and found large numbers of Haversian canals inside. They are channels that form in bone around blood vessels. Haversian canals occur today in fast-growing animals like mammals and birds, but not in reptiles like lizards. This suggested that dinosaurs grew very quickly to adulthood.

More provocatively, the study suggested that dinosaurs were warm-blooded like mammals, not cold-blooded like lizards and other reptiles as most biologists believed at the time. Later research seems to have proven that dinosaurs were warm-blooded. Studies of oxygen in *Tyrannosaurus rex* bones proved that the temperatures of these dinosaurs varied little in life, as in mammals and birds. Further evidence came in the 1990s with the discovery in China of dinosaurs with insulating coats of feathers.

▲ *This is a section through mammal bone. The hole in the center is a Haversian canal. Blood vessels run through it. They keep the living tissue of the bone supplied with oxygen and nutrients, and take away waste.*

cells are usually widely separated and are surrounded by complex mixtures of materials, such as collagen fibers. This kind of loose tissue occurs around all the organs of the body. It also connects the skin to structures directly beneath it. Denser connective tissue containing more fibers occurs where greater strength is needed, such as in ligaments and tendons. Harder types of connective tissues include cartilage and bone. Bone gets its toughness from its structure—layers of cells sandwiched between layers of tough minerals. Materials like bone are called composites.

Muscle cells

The cells of muscle tissue are able to contract (shorten) and relax, allowing movement (see 7: 40–43). Muscle cells can do this because they contain bundles of fibers that slide over one another (see 29).

THE STRUCTURE OF A NERVE CELL

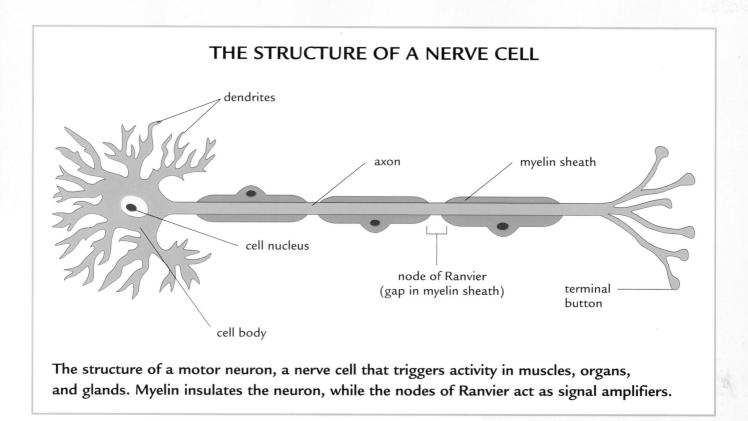

dendrites

axon

myelin sheath

cell nucleus

node of Ranvier
(gap in myelin sheath)

terminal
button

cell body

The structure of a motor neuron, a nerve cell that triggers activity in muscles, organs, and glands. Myelin insulates the neuron, while the nodes of Ranvier act as signal amplifiers.

Muscle contraction is a process that demands a lot of energy, so muscle cells are packed with mitochondria, the organelles that release energy from food (see 41–42).

Nerve cells

Nervous tissue has many densely packed nerve cells called neurons. There are at least ten billion neurons in the human brain. Neurons carry electrical signals between the brain and body. This electrical activity depends on the movement of tiny particles called ions (see 49). Each neuron consists of a central cell body that contains the nucleus (control center) and other organelles. There are several extensions of the neuron. Most cells have one long extension called an axon; they also have shorter ones called dendrites. The extensions can

CLOSEUP

GAPS IN THE MYELIN SHEATH

The myelin sheath insulates neurons against electrical interference from other nerve cells. It also prevents signals from degrading as they travel along the neuron. The sheath is peppered with gaps called nodes of Ranvier. Each gap measures less than one-thousandth of a millimeter across. Electrical impulses can jump across the gaps, allowing faster travel; in this way the nodes amplify the nerve signals.

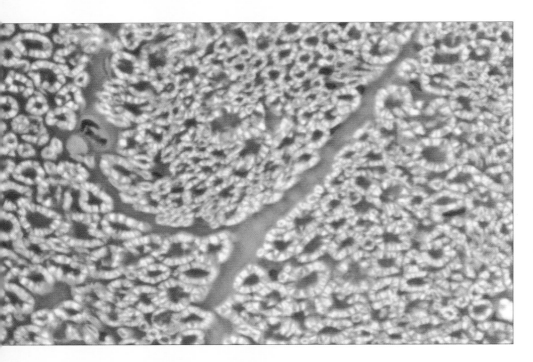

▲ *A section through brain tissue composed of neurons. Neurons carry electrical messages from the brain to the body and back.*

food reserves, fight infection, or insulate the nerve cells with fatty coatings.

The diversity of cells

Most animals have bodies composed of tissues, organs, and systems, but some have much simpler arrangements. The smallest animals, placozoans, are little more than bundles of cells. Sponges are larger, but they too do not have distinct types of tissues.

Sponges live in the ocean, attached firmly to the seabed. A system of water channels. runs through the body of a sponge. Cells with flagella line the insides of the channels. They beat their flagella to create a current that draws in fresh water from

carry electrical messages over great distances. Nervous tissue also contains supporting cells, which can be ten times more numerous than the neurons. Supporting cells store

HOT DEBATE

LEARN ABOUT STEM CELLS

Unspecialized cells in the body are called stem cells. A stem cell can become any other type of cell. Stem cells occur in embryos before the tissues and organs develop. The stem cells then begin to differentiate (specialize for certain functions). It is not just embryonic cells that differentiate. Adults also have stem cells, such as the cells that divide to become blood cells (see 60).

Stem cells can divide almost without limit and can be grown outside the body. That provides medical researchers with a window of opportunity, although the research is far from complete. For example, stem cells could be forced to differentiate into pancreas cells. They could then be implanted into the pancreas of a diabetes (see 48) sufferer. Dopamine-producing cells could treat

Parkinson's disease (see 50), while Alzheimer's, heart disease, and cancers may also become treatable.

However, adult stem cells are not ideal for medical use. Stem-cell research depends on taking cells from embryos. The embryos used are "spares" left over from IVF (see 54) programs. Stem cell research remains highly controversial, since many people think the use of these cells is abhorrent.

outside. The sponge cells then filter tiny particles of food from the water (see **6: 10**). The water current then runs out through a large opening at the top of the sponge called the osculum.

Cnidarians—a group of animals that includes corals, jellyfish, and sea anemones—have more diverse cell types. Unlike sponges, cnidarians have epithelial cells and muscle cells that help at least some of their life stages move around. However, cnidarians lack many of the cell types found in other animals, such as blood and a brain.

KILLER CNIDARIANS

Cnidarians catch and kill other animals for food. A unique type of cell called a cnidocyte helps them do this. Each cnidocyte contains a structure called a nematocyst. It is a capsule attached to a tightly coiled thread with a sharp barb at the tip. When the cnidocyte is touched by prey, a lid covering the cell pops open. The thread then explodes out of the cell, and the barb drives into the prey. Poison then goes through the barb to paralyze the prey, leaving it unable to move. The prey is then drawn into the gut for digestion.

Sea slugs are mollusks, so they are unable to produce nematocysts. However, some sea slugs take nematocysts from their prey and use them for their own defense. Aeolid sea slugs are immune to the poisons of the cnidarians they eat. The slugs store the stolen nematocysts in a pouch and use them to fend off predators.

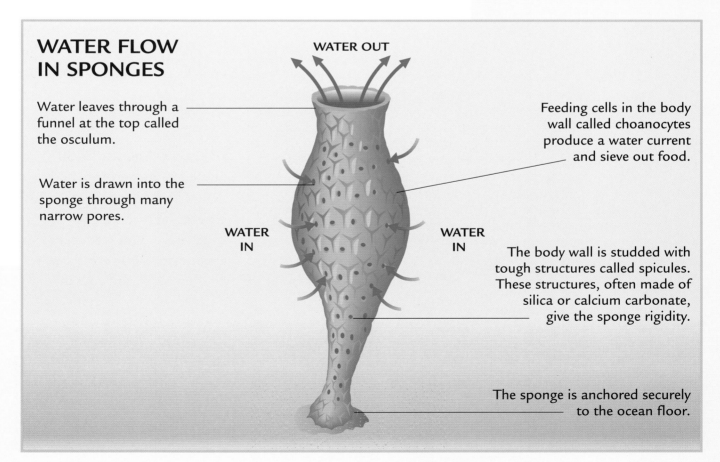

WATER FLOW IN SPONGES

WATER OUT

Water leaves through a funnel at the top called the osculum.

Water is drawn into the sponge through many narrow pores.

WATER IN

WATER IN

Feeding cells in the body wall called choanocytes produce a water current and sieve out food.

The body wall is studded with tough structures called spicules. These structures, often made of silica or calcium carbonate, give the sponge rigidity.

The sponge is anchored securely to the ocean floor.

3 Movement and Support

Cells have internal structures that support them, control their movements, and carry out functions.

▼ *Human muscle filaments. Muscle contraction involves the movement of filaments containing the proteins actin and myosin. Learn more about muscle contraction on page 29.*

Many cells have structures that allow them to move. There are also parts that move inside a cell. Other structures provide support and keep the cell's shape. An essential structure shared by all cells is the cell membrane. Surrounding the cell, it gives support as well as a barrier to the cell's environment.

An essential membrane

The cell membrane is very thin and flexible, but it is strong, like a layer of cling-wrap. It separates the inside of the cell from the outside, stops the contents from spilling free, and keeps other chemicals out. Most of the membrane is composed of complex fat molecules called phospholipids.

Cell membranes depend on the structure of phospholipids to function. Some chemicals are hydrophobic, meaning they repel water. Others attract water; they are

▶ *Different phospholipid sections respond to water in different ways. A double layer (or bilayer) can separate two water-containing areas, such as the inside and outside of a cell.*

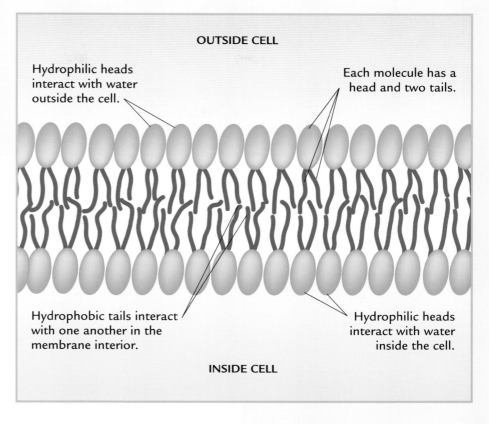

OUTSIDE CELL

Hydrophilic heads interact with water outside the cell.

Each molecule has a head and two tails.

Hydrophobic tails interact with one another in the membrane interior.

Hydrophilic heads interact with water inside the cell.

INSIDE CELL

called hydrophilic. Phospholipids are both. They have a pair of "tails" composed of fatty acids. The tails are hydrophobic, so they repel water. The "head" of a phospholipid molecule contains phosphorus; it is hydrophilic.

Phospholipids in a membrane are arranged in two layers. The tails link on the inside, while the two sets of heads pack together closely to face outward. The two layers are called the lipid bilayer.

The cell membrane gives structural support to the cell, but it is also flexible. It serves

CLOSEUP

OTHER MOLECULES IN THE MEMBRANE

The cell membrane does not consist solely of phospholipids. It is also studded with molecules called membrane proteins (right). There are usually around 25 phospholipids for each protein. Membrane proteins extend across the lipid bilayer. Like phospholipids, they have water-attracting sections extending away from the membrane and water-repelling sections that link inside it.

Some membrane proteins float around within the bilayer, although many are anchored by the cell cytoskeleton (see 24). The proteins have a range of functions, such as shuttling molecules in and out of the cell or acting as receptors for chemicals released by nerves.

The cell membrane also contains carbohydrates. They act as recognition sites for other cells, allowing the cells to stick together (see 45).

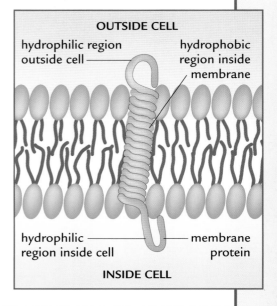

OUTSIDE CELL

hydrophilic region outside cell

hydrophobic region inside membrane

hydrophilic region inside cell

membrane protein

INSIDE CELL

HOW PLANT CELLS EXPAND

Plant cells are lined by tough banks of cellulose-rich microfibrils. How, then, do they grow? Plant cells grow when a hormone called auxin binds to receptors inside it. That makes the cell wall lose its toughness. It becomes stretchy, allowing the cell to start expanding. However, the direction of the cell's expansion depends on which way the microfibrils run around the cell wall.

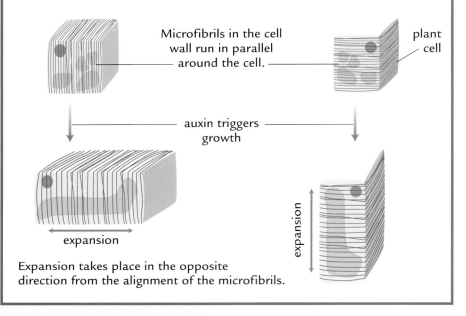

Microfibrils in the cell wall run in parallel around the cell.

plant cell

auxin triggers growth

expansion

expansion

Expansion takes place in the opposite direction from the alignment of the microfibrils.

to limit the movement of molecules in and out of the cell. Important chemicals that the cell needs to draw in or force out move through large proteins embedded in the membrane (see 21). These proteins form a series of gates and channels that allow chemical transport. Other membrane proteins provide anchorage for an internal support structure called the cytoskeleton (see 24–26).

Supporting walls

The cells of plants are more rigid than animal cells. That is because plant cells have a tough cell wall in addition to the cell membrane.

Plant cell walls consist of a type of sugar called cellulose. The cellulose is embedded in a network of other chemicals. The cell wall gets its strength from the way its cellulose molecules connect. Bundles of around 250 molecules align to form a structure called a microfibril. Other, smaller sugars form tough bridges between the microfibrils. In order to grow, cell walls must expand. A growth hormone (messenger chemical) called auxin (see **5**: 25–31) causes the cell wall to soften. It then expands in a direction determined by the way the microfibrils line up.

The cell wall is rigid, so it can resist pressure from water inside the cell. Without a cell wall the cell would burst.

THE WALLS OF BACTERIA

Like plants, bacteria have cell walls. Bacterial cell walls, though, are much more varied. Their main functions are to maintain the shape of the cell, to prevent its contents from drifting away, and to keep out unwanted chemicals. Scientists use a technique called Gram staining (see **4**: 15) to detect the presence of certain bacteria, including ones that cause disease, like *Listeria* and *Streptococcus*. Bacteria that can be detected in this way are called Gram-positive bacteria. The cell walls of Gram-positive bacteria contain large amounts of substances called peptidoglycans. They react with certain dyes to produce a deep violet color.

Antibiotics like penicillin work by disrupting bacterial cell walls. Once its cell wall is breached, a bacterium cannot retain the concentrated soup of chemicals its needs to function, and it dies.

Instead, it becomes rigid, like a balloon filling with air. That allows well-watered plants to grow tall and strong even if they do not contain hard woody tissues.

Cell junctions

Cell membranes and walls connect cells to their neighbors. There are several types of cell junctions. Chemical messages go from cell to cell through gap junctions (see 46–47). Tight junctions prevent molecules moving along the spaces between cells.

Desmosomes are junctions that provide structural support. They occur in epithelial tissues, which lie on the outside of body surfaces, forming the skin or wall of the gut, for example. Desmosomes are very tough joints. Proteins called keratin extend through the cell cytoplasm from desmosome to desmosome. Keratin also forms structures such as the fingernails.

▼ *A desmosome, a tough type of joint that links two cells. Desmosomes occur in the skin and other places of regular wear and tear.*

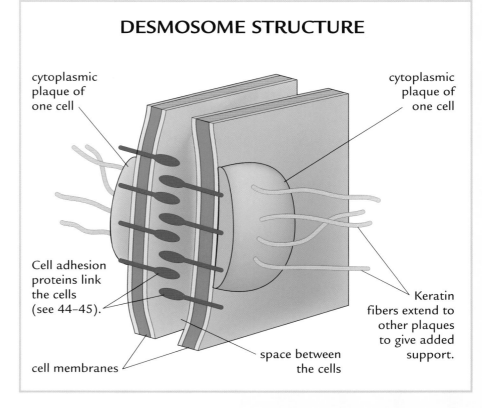

DESMOSOME STRUCTURE

cytoplasmic plaque of one cell

cytoplasmic plaque of one cell

Cell adhesion proteins link the cells (see 44–45).

Keratin fibers extend to other plaques to give added support.

cell membranes

space between the cells

THE MITOTIC SPINDLE

One of the best-known microtubule functions is the formation of the spindle during cell division (see **3**: 16–25). The spindle is a set of microtubules that appears when a cell is ready to divide.

First, microtubules of the regular cytoskeleton break down. Units of tubulin are then reassembled into a structure shaped like a birdcage. That is the spindle. It grows longer and longer, forcing the cell to stretch. At the same time, molecules of DNA (which carry genetic information) coil to form chromatids, which pair up to form structures called chromosomes. Microtubules from the ends of the spindle attach to the chromosomes. The microtubules then shorten, pulling each chromatid from its partner, which is pulled in the opposite direction. Once the DNA is divided, the cell divides, and the spindle disintegrates. A new cytoskeleton then forms in each of the new cells.

INSIDE THE CELL

Prokaryotes (see 7) depend on the cell wall and membrane for support. Eukaryote cells such as those of animals and plants contain a network of fibers that provides support. It is called the cytoskeleton. It criss-crosses the cytoplasm (see 31–32) and underpins the cell membrane. There are three main types of fibers in the cytoskeleton. They are microtubules, actin filaments, and intermediate filaments.

Microtubules

The largest fibers in a cell's cytoskeleton are the microtubules. At 25 nanometers across, these fibers are just large enough to be seen with an ordinary light microscope.

Microtubules have a diverse range of functions. They are hollow tubes made of a protein called tubulin. Every microtubule contains 13 tiny filaments. They weave together to make the complete fiber. The fiber can be lengthened or shortened by adding or taking away tubulin molecules.

MICROTUBULE STRUCTURE

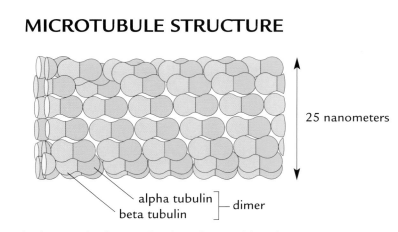

25 nanometers

alpha tubulin ⎤ dimer
beta tubulin ⎦

Microtubules are hollow cylinders formed by the protein tubulin. There are two types of tubulins, alpha and beta, that link together to form a molecule called a dimer. Microtubules grow or shorten by the addition or removal of dimers.

NANOMETERS

A nanometer is a tiny measurement indeed. It is equal to one billionth of a meter, or around one 25-millionth of an inch.

Understanding actin

At just 7 nanometers across, microfilaments are the smallest of the fibers that occur in the cytoskeleton. They are made of a protein called actin. A microfilament consists of two actin polymers (long chains; see **1**: 30) that are twisted together to form a helix, or spiral, shape. Just like microtubules, microfilaments can be rapidly lengthened or shortened by adding or taking away actin molecules. That is important for changing the cell's shape and for generating movement (see 29).

Actin is one of the most abundant proteins in an animal's body. Almost 10 percent of your soft tissues (excluding water) is actin.

Intermediate filaments

Intermediate filaments are somewhere between microtubules and microfilaments in diameter. They are different from other cytoskeletal fibers

---

FILAMENTS OF THE CYTOSKELETON

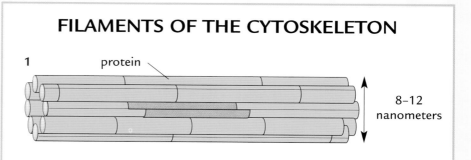

1   protein

8–12 nanometers

Intermediate filaments (**1**) are made of fibers of proteins that are bound into a ropelike structure. That gives the cell strength and helps it keep its shape.

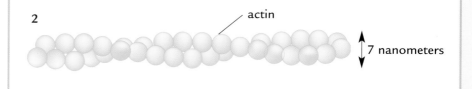

2   actin

7 nanometers

Microfilaments (**2**) are made of actin. They can change shape to drive movement of other cellular structures. Microfilaments and myosin work together to allow muscle contraction (see 29).

---

because their exact composition varies with the type of cell. Intermediate filaments

INTERMEDIATE FILAMENT TYPING

Intermediate filaments from different tissues vary in their chemical makeup. Six types of intermediate filament proteins occur in animals. Usually only one occurs in any one tissue type. Scientists can find out the tissue in which a cell originated by studying the intermediate filaments inside. That is called intermediate filament, or IF, typing. IF typing is of great importance in the fight against cancer. Cancer tumors can quickly spread around the body. By looking at the intermediate filaments of a cancerous cell, scientists can decide where in the body the cancer started. That helps doctors target treatments more effectively.

AMAZING AMEBOID LOCOMOTION

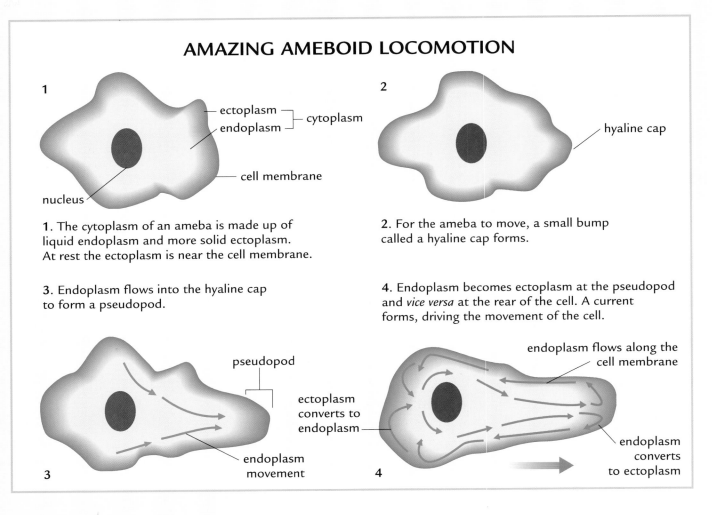

1

ectoplasm
endoplasm — cytoplasm

cell membrane

nucleus

1. The cytoplasm of an ameba is made up of liquid endoplasm and more solid ectoplasm. At rest the ectoplasm is near the cell membrane.

2

hyaline cap

2. For the ameba to move, a small bump called a hyaline cap forms.

3. Endoplasm flows into the hyaline cap to form a pseudopod.

4. Endoplasm becomes ectoplasm at the pseudopod and *vice versa* at the rear of the cell. A current forms, driving the movement of the cell.

pseudopod

ectoplasm converts to endoplasm

endoplasm movement

3

endoplasm flows along the cell membrane

endoplasm converts to ectoplasm

4

FINDING FLAGELLA

You can see cells moving with an ordinary light microscope, the kind in your school biology lab. Take a sample of ordinary pond water, and see if you can spot some single-celled organisms. How do they move? See if you can figure out whether the creatures are using cilia, flagella, or ameboid locomotion to swim around.

are also more stable and form a permanent scaffold inside the cell—their sole function is to provide internal support. Intermediate filaments give cells their strength.

MOVEMENT

As well as providing structural support, the cytoskeletal proteins play an important role in the movement of cells as well as whole organisms. Other types of proteins, such as myosin and dynein, are also important for movement.

How amebas move around

Amebas are protists (a group of single-celled organisms; see **4**: 20–31) that move around in an incredible way. The cytoplasm of an ameba contains a liquid, endoplasm, that is usually near the center of the cell. The cytoplasm also contains a more solid substance, ectoplasm, that lies close to the cell membrane. For the cell to move, the ectoplasm pushes out to form a bump. The endoplasm then begins to

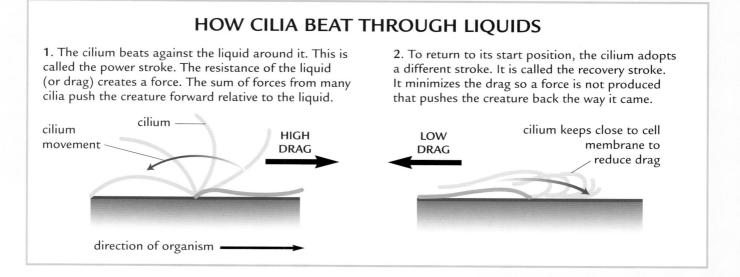

HOW CILIA BEAT THROUGH LIQUIDS

1. The cilium beats against the liquid around it. This is called the power stroke. The resistance of the liquid (or drag) creates a force. The sum of forces from many cilia push the creature forward relative to the liquid.

2. To return to its start position, the cilium adopts a different stroke. It is called the recovery stroke. It minimizes the drag so a force is not produced that pushes the creature back the way it came.

cilium
movement

cilium

HIGH DRAG

LOW DRAG

cilium keeps close to cell membrane to reduce drag

direction of organism

---

flow into the bump. This forms an extension called a pseudopod, or "false foot." As the liquid endoplasm reaches the false foot, it is converted into more solid ectoplasm and runs back along the cell membrane.

At the same time, the opposite takes place at the rear of the ameba. There ectoplasm changes to endoplasm, which flows through the cell to the false foot. In this way the ameba slowly inches forward. Biologists call this type of movement ameboid locomotion.

Cilia and flagella
Many protists use ameboid locomotion to get around. Others use a more active system. These creatures move by using cilia (sing. cilium) or flagella (sing. flagellum). Cilia

and flagella are tail-like extensions of cells. Flagella are long and move in a whip-like fashion. Usually there are just one or two on a cell. A wave runs down the flagellum, driving the cell along. Cilia are shorter and usually occur in much greater numbers. Individual cilia are less effective than a flagellum; but

▲ *Cilia can move a tiny creature through water or help move a liquid, such as mucus, in a larger animal.*

▼ *How a flagellum, such as one on a sperm, pushes a cell forward through a liquid.*

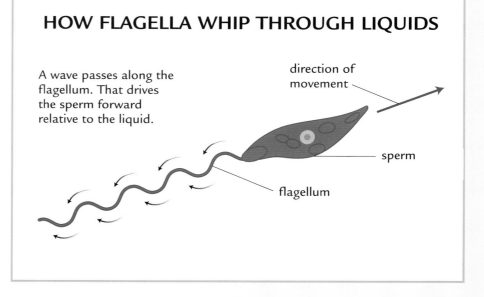

HOW FLAGELLA WHIP THROUGH LIQUIDS

A wave passes along the flagellum. That drives the sperm forward relative to the liquid.

direction of movement

sperm

flagellum

THE FLAGELLA OF BACTERIA

Many bacteria also have flagella. However, they are very different from those of eukaryotes such as protists, suggesting that their flagella evolved independently. Bacterial flagella do not have microtubule doublets or even dynein. They are made of a different protein, flagellin. Bacterial flagella do not have waves of motion; instead, they spin around like an airplane propeller.

when they beat in concert with many others, they make good oars. Cilia move in a way similar to a swimmer doing the breaststroke; a power stroke is followed by a recovery stroke, in which the cilium keeps as close to the cell membrane as possible.

How cilia and flagella work

Cilia and flagella anchor onto the cytoskeleton. Although they look different, their internal structures and the way they power their movements are the same. A cilium consists of nine pairs (or doublets) of tiny tubes called microtubules. One of each pair is complete; the other is incomplete and is fused to its partner. The doublets are arranged in a circle to form a larger tubular structure.

The doublets surround a single central pair of tubules, which are bound by a sheath. Biologists call this the "9 + 2" arrangement. Nine protein spokes radiate from the sheath to the outer pairs. Movement depends on the doublets sliding past each other. To do this a motor protein called dynein is needed.

INSIDE A CILIUM

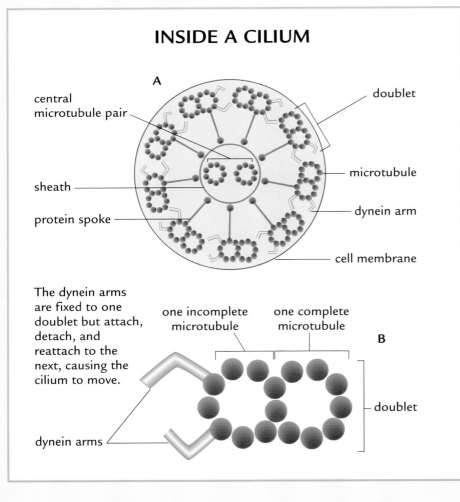

central microtubule pair

doublet

sheath

microtubule

protein spoke

dynein arm

cell membrane

The dynein arms are fixed to one doublet but attach, detach, and reattach to the next, causing the cilium to move.

one incomplete microtubule

one complete microtubule

B

doublet

dynein arms

A cross-section through a cilium (A) shows the 9 + 2 arrangement of microtubules. B shows a doublet and the motor protein, dynein, in greater detail.

Dynein forms "arms" on each doublet that attach to the next doublet along. A chemical called ATP changes the shape of a dynein arm. That makes the next doublet move.

Many tiny creatures use cilia for propulsion. The largest ciliated animals, comb jellies, are around 0.5 inches (1.25cm) across. Movement using cilia is inefficient for larger animals, but cilia are still important for moving things around inside the body. For example, mucus in the windpipe is moved along by beating banks of cilia. Similarly, animal sperm swims by using flagella. For the whole animal to move, though, muscle is needed.

Mighty muscles

Muscle function is similar to ciliary movement, since filaments attach and reattach to slide across each other. Muscle is formed of bundles of fibers called myofibrils.

Each contains sections called sarcomeres. They are made of actin microfilaments that overlap with filaments of another protein, myosin. Myosin filaments are thick, and each is surrounded by six thinner actin microfilaments.

To contract the muscle, nervous signals cause the release of calcium ions (see 49). That triggers the myosin molecules to attach to actin. The attachment causes the filaments to move a little (around 10 nanometers). An ATP molecule then binds to the myosin, making it release the actin. The myosin is now ready to reattach to the actin. By repeating this cycle many times, the sarcomere shortens, and the muscle contracts.

RIGIDITY OF DEATH

When an organism dies, its muscles soon stiffen. This is called rigor mortis. Death stops the transport of ATP into muscles. The bonds between actin and myosin cannot be broken, so the muscles stiffen. Eventually the proteins begin to break down, and the muscle softens. These events take place on a predictable timescale. Police scientists study the stiffness of a corpse in a homicide enquiry. That can help the scientists establish the time that has passed since the victim's death.

▶ *The structure of a myofibril in detail. Sarcomeres are the units that contract to make muscles move. Light filaments in the sarcomere contain actin; darker filaments are composed of myosin.*

sarcomere

4 Inside the Cell

▼ *An animal cell. The nucleus controls all cell activities. It controls what proteins are made. Cytoplasm is the cell's contents outside the nucleus, including organelles (see 33–39). Most organelles are involved with making, processing, packaging, and transporting proteins. Mitochondria produce energy.*

Cells can be described as factories. Each has the machinery needed to perform its own particular tasks and keep itself healthy.

The internal structure of cells varies with cell type and function. The greatest differences are those between prokaryotic and eukaryotic cells. Prokaryotes (bacteria, see **4**: 8–19) are generally smaller and simpler.

Eukaryotic cells are highly compartmentalized—most of their essential functions occur inside specialized structures enclosed by membranes. Like the organs of organisms such as multicellular plants and animals, each of these so-called "organelles" performs a particular task.

In prokaryotic cells there is much less organization: They contain deoxyribonucleic acid (DNA; see **4**: 14) but no internal membranes. The only structures prokaryotic cells have in common with eukaryotic cells are the external cell

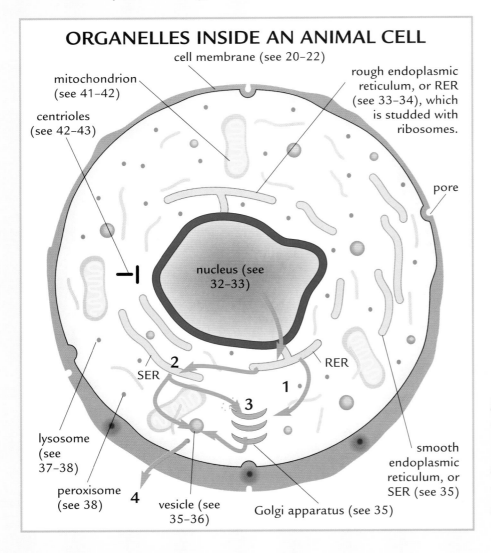

ORGANELLES INSIDE AN ANIMAL CELL

cell membrane (see 20–22)

mitochondrion (see 41–42)

centrioles (see 42–43)

rough endoplasmic reticulum, or RER (see 33–34), which is studded with ribosomes.

pore

nucleus (see 32–33)

2

SER

1

3

RER

lysosome (see 37–38)

peroxisome (see 38)

4

vesicle (see 35–36)

Golgi apparatus (see 35)

smooth endoplasmic reticulum, or SER (see 35)

◀ *Red arrows trace some protein-production paths. mRNA (see 33) brings instructions from the nucleus to RER (1), where ribosomes make proteins. Vesicles carry proteins to SER (2) or the Golgi apparatus (3) for processing and then, perhaps, the cell membrane for export (4).*

membrane and internal structures called ribosomes (see 34). They have no organelles.

Protoplasm, cytoplasm, and cytosol

"Protoplasm" is a rather outdated word for the contents of a cell. Biologists now know that protoplasm is far from the uniform mass it was once described as. *Cytoplasm* is now used to describe the contents of the cell outside the nucleus, including organelles.

Textbook diagrams of cells usually show the various internal structures or organelles floating in a jellylike fluid, the cytosol, which also contains the cytoskeleton (see 24–26). The cytosol is a rich soup of chemical compounds. It is also the site of many cellular reactions. The cytoplasm itself is extremely

▶ *Skin cells called melanocytes contain pigments (molecules that produce color). Vitiligo occurs when melanocytes lose their ability to make pigments. Patches of the skin lose their color, and the normal skin color rarely returns. There is no cure.*

THE ORIGIN OF CELLS

The word "nucleolus" was first used by the German biologists Matthias Schleiden (1804–1881) and Theodor Schwann (1810–1882). They noted the similarities between plant and animals cells, and popularized cell theory, which states that living things are all made up of cells.

Schleiden and Schwann believed that cells are made from a mass of structureless jelly called cytoblastema. The first stage in the development of a cell, they said, was the appearance of a tiny dark granule, the nucleolus. The nucleus and then the cell itself build up layer by layer around this tiny core. We now know that this idea was wrong, and that all cells form by division (see 52–61). The nucleolus (see 33), which does exist, has kept its name, though.

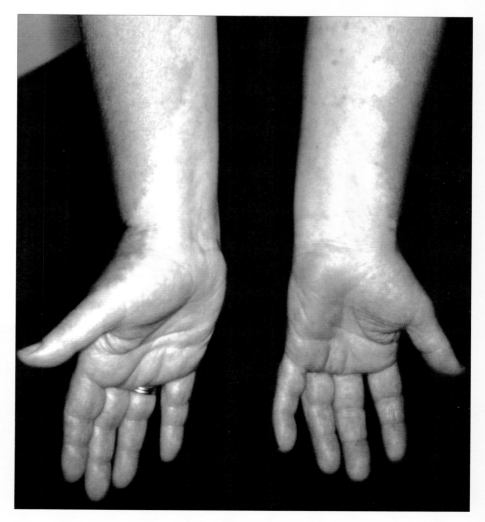

complex. It incorporates the cytoskeleton, a supportive network of minute tubes and threads, and the cytosol as well as organelles (see 33–43).

ORGANELLES
The nucleus

The nucleus is the largest organelle in a eukaryotic cell. It can be seen under a relatively low-powered microscope, often without special treatment. The nucleus is bound by a double membrane called the nuclear envelope. The nuclear envelope is perforated by numerous openings or pores. They allow messenger molecules (see 44–51) to move in and out of the nucleus.

The messenger molecules carry instructions regarding the manufacture of essential

MULTINUCLEATE CELLS

Most cells have just one nucleus, but many single-celled protists (see **4**: 20–31) are multinucleate—they have many nuclei. For example, amebas such as *Chaos* (below) can have several nuclei. Ciliate protists like *Paramecium* have two types of nuclei, one large (the macronucleus) and one small (the micronucleus). Multinucleate cells also occur in some animal tissues, including certain muscle tissues.

cell components and molecules, such as enzymes. The nucleus of most cells also has an area called the nucleolus dedicated to the production of ribosomes (see 34).

In every body cell the nucleus contains a full copy of the organism's genes (units of inherited information). Genes are segments of a molecule called deoxyribonucleic acid, or DNA (see **3**: 26–37). When a cell is not dividing, DNA forms tiny, invisible threads called chromatin. As a cell prepares to divide (see 55–56), the DNA copies itself. Then the chromatin coils to form chromosomes, which are divided between the two new daughter cells. Chromosomes unwind back into chromatin.

When a cell is not dividing, there is still plenty of activity inside the nucleus. For instance, the strands of DNA are used as templates to make messenger ribonucleic acid, or mRNA (see **3**: 32–35). In this way mRNA carries the genetic code on DNA from the nucleus to the rest of the cell. There the information on mRNA directs the production of proteins such as hormones and enzymes (see **1**: 28–37).

Rough endoplasmic reticulum (RER)

The grandly named rough endoplasmic reticulum, or RER, surrounds the nucleus and is connected to the nuclear envelope. The RER's

Rough endoplasmic reticulum (RER) is connected to the nuclear envelope.

nuclear envelope

animal cell

nucleus

ROUGH ENDOPLASMIC RETICULUM

This surface connects to the nuclear envelope.

rough endoplasmic reticulum

ribosomes

smooth endoplasmic reticulum (not attached to the nucleus)

Rough endoplasmic reticulum (RER) is made up of many folded membranes. Ribosomes attached to the RER give it a rough surface. They are the sites for protein manufacture.

SMOOTH ENDOPLASMIC RETICULUM

Smooth endoplasmic reticulum is not connected to the nuclear envelope.

nucleus

nuclear envelope

cell

There are no ribosomes on smooth endoplasmic reticulum (SER). Proteins made on the RER are processed by the SER.

size varies, but it is largest in cells that manufacture large quantities of proteins. The word *reticulum* means "network" and refers to the complex shape of the RER. *Endoplasmic* describes the organelle's location in the cell (*endo* means "inside"). *Rough* refers to the fact that the outer membranes of RER are studded all over with tiny granular strucures called ribosomes (see box below left).

RER is like a processing and manufacturing plant where the instructions coded on DNA in the nucleus are put into action. Ribosomes use strands of messenger RNA (made from DNA) to join amino acids into chains (see **3**: 33). These chains, called polypeptides (see **1**: 33) are made into proteins. The newly made proteins accumulate inside the RER. They are then packaged and transferred to the Golgi apparatus (see 35) for further processing.

CLOSEUP

RIBOSOMES

Strictly speaking, ribosomes are not organelles because they are not bound by membranes. They are the only internal cell structure that occurs in both prokaryotic and eukaryotic cells. Ribosomes are either free in the cytosol or attached to the membranes of rough endoplasmic reticulum (which only occurs in eukaryote cells). Their job is to "read" the genetic instructions coded on strands of messenger RNA (see **3**: 32–35). They build the various proteins needed by the cell. Ribosomes are small—those of eukaryotic cells are about 30 nm in diameter, and prokaryotic ribosomes are even smaller.

THE GOLGI APPARATUS

The Golgi appartatus is an organelle that modifies and packages most of the molecules made by RER and SER. It was discovered by the Italian physician Camillo Golgi (1844–1926) and now bears his name. The apparatus is a stack of disk-shaped sacs called cisternae. Each stack has two "faces," the cis and the trans. Each side, or face, contains different enzymes. Proteins arrive at the cis side. Enzymes then activate them within the Golgi apparatus. Processed molecules then leave in small vesicles (sacs) pinched off from the trans side of the stack. The vesicles transport the proteins to wherever they are needed. Some travel to the cell membrane for export, others are needed inside the cell.

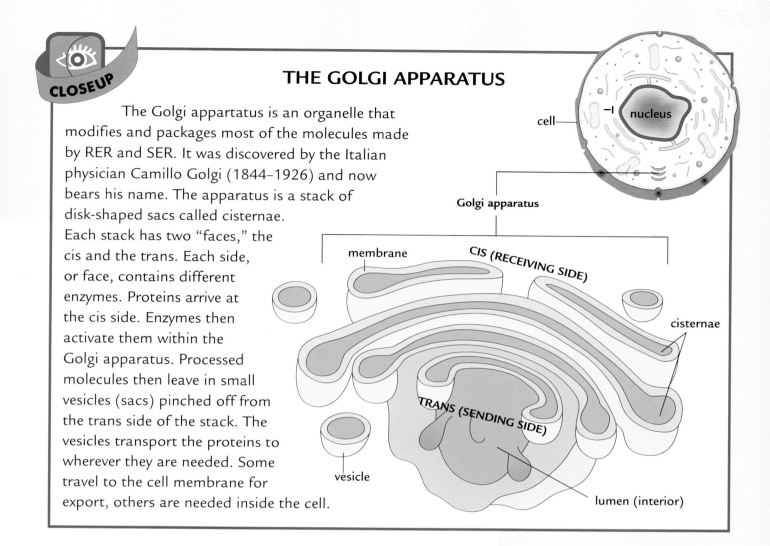

cell — nucleus

Golgi apparatus

membrane

CIS (RECEIVING SIDE)

cisternae

TRANS (SENDING SIDE)

vesicle

lumen (interior)

Smooth endoplasmic reticulum (SER)

Smooth endoplasmic reticulum, SER, has no ribosomes and is not attached to the nuclear envelope. SER has a tubular structure and forms stacks of flattened sacs, like piles of fat pancakes riddled with holes (see 34).

SER packages proteins that are due to be exported from the cell, such as secretory proteins. It is the site of synthesis for various lipids (see **1**: 32).

Vacuoles and vesicles

Also present in the cytoplasm of plant and animal cells is an assortment of membrane-bound organelles called vacuoles and vesicles. They are mainly used for storage or transport of food, waste, or various kinds of molecules made in the cell.

Vacuoles are generally temporary structures that form by budding off other membranes (in particular, the cell membrane, RER, SER, and Golgi

ENDOCYTOSIS AND EXOCYTOSIS

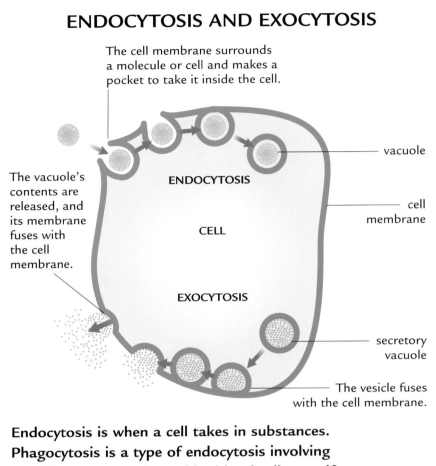

The cell membrane surrounds a molecule or cell and makes a pocket to take it inside the cell.

The vacuole's contents are released, and its membrane fuses with the cell membrane.

ENDOCYTOSIS

vacuole

cell membrane

CELL

EXOCYTOSIS

secretory vacuole

The vesicle fuses with the cell membrane.

Endocytosis is when a cell takes in substances. Phagocytosis is a type of endocytosis involving particles, such as when white blood cells engulf foreign bodies. Pinocytosis is when a cell takes in liquids. Exocytosis is the process cells use to get rid of substances.

apparatus). Vacuoles are reabsorbed into the membrane and recycled once their job is done.

When vacuoles form from the cell membrane to bring some substance into the cell, the process is called endocytosis. The reverse process, by which vacuoles fuse with the cell membrane in order to eject their contents from the cell, is exocytosis (see left).

Contractile vacuole

Aquatic protozoa, including ciliates, flagellates, and amebas (see **4: 22**), have a contractile vacuole. It acts like an organ for expelling excess water. The contents of a freshwater protozoan cell are more concentrated than the medium in which the organism lives. This means there is a constant tendency for water to enter the cell by osmosis. To prevent the cytoplasm from

TRY THIS

CONTRACTILE VACUOLES

Use a microscope to examine a freshwater protozoan such as *Paramecium* mounted in a drop of fresh water under a coverslip. Look around the cell edge for a round vacuole that gradually increases in size, then suddenly disappears.

It is a contractile vacuole (*Paramecium* have two). Using a stopwatch, time how long it takes the vacuole to expand and discharge 10 times, then figure out an average. Using a fine pipette, transfer the organism to a 2 percent solution of salt water

(2 grams salt in 98 ml fresh water). Time 10 cycles. Repeat the process with 4, 6, and 8 percent salt solutions. Compare your results. Using water that contains more salt means there is less difference in concentration between the cell and its environment.

becoming dangerously diluted, or even exploding, the organism must actively expel water.

The contractile vacuole absorbs water from the cytoplasm, expanding as it fills, then fuses with the cell membrane and expels water.

Lysosomes

Lysosomes are a feature of animal cells. They contain several different digestive enzymes that break down large molecules such as proteins, fats, and carbohydrates. Such molecules are taken into the cell by phagocytosis (see 36).

Lysosomes digest dead or unwanted material and appear to play an important role in recycling materials when cells die. Lysosomes are usually 0.5-1.0 µm in diameter and are enveloped in a single layer of membrane. The digestive enzymes are manufactured on the rough endoplasmic reticulum, from where they are transferred to the Golgi apparatus. New lysosomes that have recently budded off the Golgi apparatus are called primary lysosomes. They become secondary lysosomes when they have fused with a vacuole and have begun breaking down the contents.

The products of lysosome digestion are tiny molecules such as amino acids. They are small enough to move across

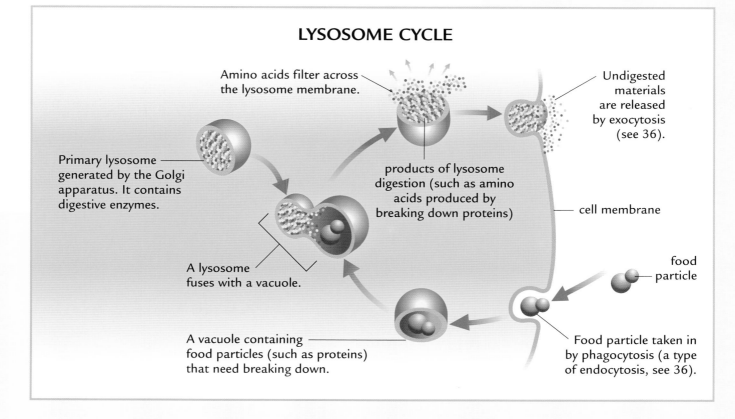

LYSOSOME CYCLE

Amino acids filter across the lysosome membrane.

Undigested materials are released by exocytosis (see 36).

Primary lysosome generated by the Golgi apparatus. It contains digestive enzymes.

products of lysosome digestion (such as amino acids produced by breaking down proteins)

cell membrane

food particle

A lysosome fuses with a vacuole.

A vacuole containing food particles (such as proteins) that need breaking down.

Food particle taken in by phagocytosis (a type of endocytosis, see 36).

PLANT VACUOLES

One of the most distinctive features of plant cells, apart from the cell wall (see 11), is the vacuole, a large, apparently empty space in the middle.

A vacuole contains mostly water, and it is important in keeping plant tissues rigid. As long as the plant is kept well watered, the vacuole remains inflated.

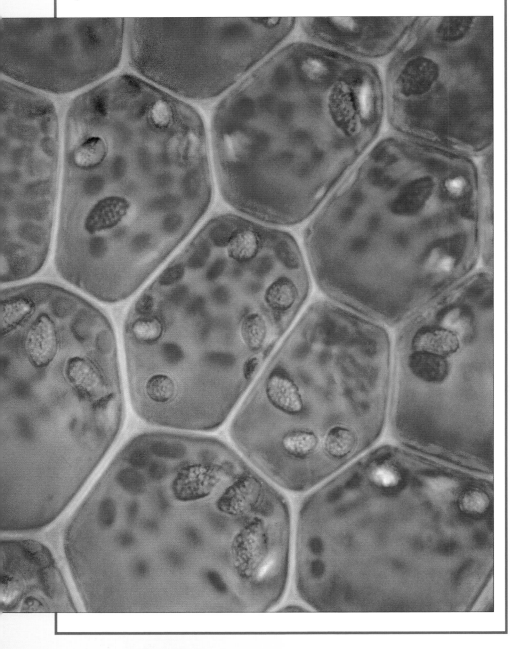

the lysosome membrane and into the cytosol. Amino acids are then used to make proteins. Any indigestible material still in the lysosome is eventually expelled from the cell when the organelle fuses with the cell membrane.

Peroxisomes

Peroxisomes are small organelles (0.5-1.0 μm) enclosed by membranes. Peroxisomes are similar to lysosomes and occur in both plant and animal cells. They have several functions, including packaging and breaking down poisons such as hydrogen peroxide, methanol, and other potentially harmful substances.

In animal cells peroxisomes assist in the chemical changes of certain fatty acids that cannot be effectively processed by other organelles. In plant cells peroxisomes are usually associated with mitochondria and chloroplasts. They are also involved in

DISCOVERY OF LYSOSOMES

Lysosomes were not discovered by microscopy but by biochemistry. In the 1950s cell biologist Christian de Duve (born 1917) was conducting experiments on the action of the hormone insulin. He noticed that some extracts of liver tissue were being digested by enzymes that appeared when the tissues were ground up. He thought that the enzymes must be leaking from mystery vesicles that ruptured during the preparation process. Later de Duve traced the source of the enzymes to a previously undescribed class of organelle, which he called lysosomes (from the Greek *lysis*, meaning "breakdown" or "digestion"). In 1974 de Duve won a Nobel Prize for his work.

chemical changes, including converting stored fats into useful carbohydrates.

Chloroplasts

The term chloroplast means "green particle." These prominent organelles give green plants their color. Chloroplasts belong to a group of organelles generally called plastids. In plants such as copper beeches, red sycamores, and in red and brown seaweeds the plastids contain other pigments that mask the underlying green color. These plastids are called chromoplasts (colored particles).

Chloroplasts are large—often up to 10 μm long. They occur in all photosynthetic cells, from tiny single-celled algae such as *Chlamydomonas* to the cells that form the leaves of tall trees. There may be just one or many

ATP AND A CHLOROPLAST

Chloroplasts capture the energy of sunlight and store it in molecules of the compound adenosine triphosphate (ATP). ATP is made in the thylakoid membranes of chloroplasts (**1**). ATP is used to make sugars in the stroma (**2**). Both these reactions make up the process of photosynthesis.

When ATP is converted to adenosine diphosphate (ADP), it releases a burst of energy that fuels cellular activity. ADP changes back to ATP in respiration (see **1**: 34). In this process glucose and oxygen react to form water and carbon dioxide, along with the release of energy.

1. Thylakoid membranes are where the green pigment chlorophyll uses light energy to make ATP. This is called the "light reaction" stage of photosynthesis.

2. Stroma is the space inside a chloroplast. It is a solution of enzymes. Using the energy stored in ATP, the enzymes turn carbon dioxide into sugars during photosynthesis. This is called the "dark reaction" stage of photosynthesis.

A granum is a stack of thylakoids.

inner membrane

outer membrane

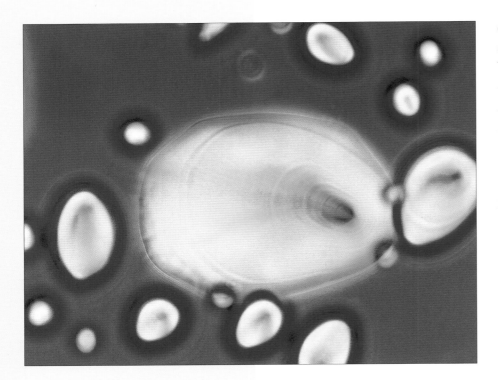

▲ *Leucoplasts are organelles in the cells of a potato. They act as stores for starch granules, shown here magnified 400 times.*

chloroplasts per cell. Each is enclosed in a double membrane layer and has a complex arrangement of flattened sacs called thylakoids. Thylakoids contain chlorophyll. They are arranged in interconnected stacks called grana (sing. granum) and are surrounded by a fluid called the stroma.

It is impossible to overstate the importance of chloroplasts to life on Earth. They are the site of photosynthesis (see **5**: 7), the process by which plants use sunlight to make carbohydrates (the chemical fuel used by all cells) from carbon dioxide and water. Photosynthesis is the basis of the food chain in which plants become food for animals (see **9**: 5).

In addition to photosynthesis chloroplasts often also have a role in storing starch granules or lipid droplets. Some plants have plastids called leucoplasts, which store starch granules.

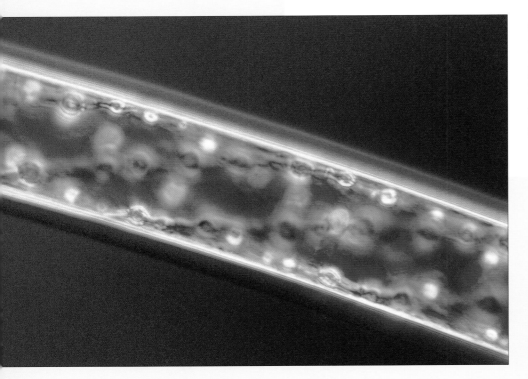

◄ *Green chloroplasts can be seen in this strand of green alga (Sprirogyra), magnified 400 times.*

Mitochondria

After the nucleus, mitochondria (sing. mitochondrion) are usually the next most conspicuous features of animal and fungal cells. Other eukaryotes such as plants and seaweeds have them too, but they are often dwarfed by chloroplasts.

Mitochondria are large—usually a few microns in length, about the size of a bacterial cell. Their structure is very distinctive (see below). They are bound by a double-layered membrane. The outer layer of the membrane is relatively smooth, enclosing the organelle in a fairly regular oval shape. The inner

MITOCHONDRIAL EVE

Mitochondria contain small amounts of DNA that replicate (copy themselves) independently of DNA in the nucleus. Mitochondrial DNA (mDNA) is unique because plants and animals inherit it all from their female parent (see **3**: 48–49). Differences in mDNA sequences between generations can only occur by random mutations (changes). Such mutations are rare, but reasonably constant. It has thus been possible to measure the amount of differences in mDNA. This provides a kind of molecular clock for estimating the number of generations and therefore the time that must have elapsed since two or more individuals had a common (female) ancestor.

The technique has been used to suggest that the most recent common ancestor (through the female line) of all humans alive on Earth today was a woman who lived in Africa about 200,000 years ago. This woman is known as Mitochondrial Eve.

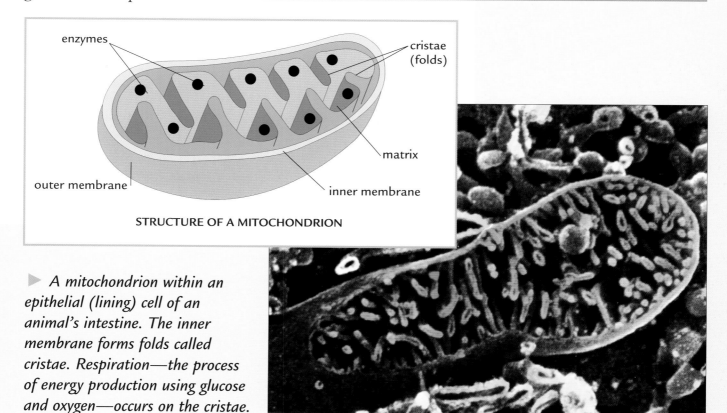

STRUCTURE OF A MITOCHONDRION

▶ A mitochondrion within an epithelial (lining) cell of an animal's intestine. The inner membrane forms folds called cristae. Respiration—the process of energy production using glucose and oxygen—occurs on the cristae.

ENERGY FROM FOOD

You will need: unsalted peanuts, a coffee pot holder (or large can), a lighter or matches, a small ringpull can, foil, scissors, a jar with a lid, a cooking thermometer, water, tape.

1 Wrap foil around the coffee-pot holder on either side of the handle. Tape the edges together to form a tube. Fold the ends of the tube neatly. Cut two slots in the foil near the top of the pot.

2 Fill a clean, empty ringpull can with water. Measure its temperature with a cooking thermometer. Now place a peanut on the lid of the small jar.

3 With the help of an adult, light the peanut with a match or lighter. Then slot the coffee-pot holder or large can over the lit peanut with the base uppermost.

1

SAFETY NOTE

Be very careful if you use matches or a lighter. Always ask an adult to help you.

Now rest the small can of water on top, on the base of the coffee-pot holder.

Once the peanut burns out, use the thermometer to test the temperature of the water in the can. The water should now be much warmer, showing the peanut has given out real heat energy.

3

Food provides energy for animals. They need it to keep warm and for movement. Energy release occurs by a chemical change when cells "burn" food fuel. Foods like peanuts are high in energy.

membrane is highly folded and forms a series of layers called cristae.

Mitochondria are the cell's power plants. Inside them cellular fuels such as sugars and fats are converted into useful chemical energy. The most important product of the process is the energy-storage compound adenosine triphosphate (ATP). ATP is a molecule that readily converts to adenosine diphosphate (ADP). Simultaneously it releases a burst of heat energy. ATP produced by mitochondria is collected by other cell components that need energy to perform their various functions.

Centrioles

Eukaryotic cells except flowering plants, pine trees, and some protists contain a structure called the centrosome. It is positioned near the nucleus It contains a pair of rodlike structures called centrioles. In

LORENZO'S OIL

The sex-linked disease adreoleukodystrophy, or ALD, affects young boys. It was brought to the world's attention by the 1992 movie *Lorenzo's Oil*. It showed the efforts of Augusto and Michaela Odone to find a treatment for their son Lorenzo, who was dying from ALD. ALD is a disease caused by the failure of peroxisomes to chemically change certain fatty acids. The treatment Lorenzo's parents discovered was another fatty acid, now called Lorenzo's oil, that may stop the progress of the disease when taken as part of a strictly controlled low-fat diet. The treatment is still controversial because scientists are still not sure precisely how or if it works.

turn the centrioles are made of microtubules (see 24). In cell division centrioles have a role in the formation of the mitotic spindle, which chromosomes are moved around by (see 24).

◄ *While exercising, cells in the human body burn up food. A chemical change occurs during which energy and warmth are released. Sweating helps cool the body down again.*

5 Cell Communication

Communication inside and between cells is vital for the smooth running of an organism's various body systems.

Your body is made up of cells that form tissues. They are groups of cooperating cells that share a common function. Tissues make up organs, such as the stomach, liver, or kidneys. For a cell to function correctly, different parts of it need to communicate. Similarly, all the cells within an organ must be in contact with each other so they can work together. Cells also need to send and receive information to and from organs such as the brain. Signals can be of two types. Some are chemical messages that trigger responses in other cells. Other messages take the form of electrical impulses.

Getting organized

In multicellular (many-celled) creatures such as people it is vital that cells in a tissue can recognize each other. Cell surfaces contain a chemical called a cell adhesion molecule, or CAM. The CAM allows the cell to stick only to similar cell types. For

▼ *Cell communication is essential for the well-being of the body. Sometimes communication breaks down, as in the disease diabetes (see 48). Diabetics must check their blood-sugar levels regularly. Here a diabetic tests for sugar in blood drawn from a prick in the finger.*

example, a CAM enables liver cells to attach only to other liver cells. That keeps all the cells in a tissue organized and prevents other cell types from getting in the way.

Types of junctions

Adjacent cells are linked by several types of cell junctions. Tight junctions occur in the layers of cells that surround body cavities like the gut. Formed by the binding of proteins that extend out from inside the cells, tight junctions prevent even tiny molecules from passing between the cells. So a molecule moving from the gut of an animal into its bloodstream must go into the cells of the gut wall first. Tight junctions stop the molecule from slipping through the spaces in between.

HOW DO CELLS STICK TOGETHER?

It is well-known that if a sponge is mashed up and run through a sieve, the cells will join again to re-form a complete sponge. How do sponges manage this neat trick? Sponge cells have molecules (called CAMs) of a protein protruding from their surfaces. When two proteins come into contact, they bind, joining the cells. That allows the sponge to re-form.

Sponges have no organs. But similar proteins allow cells to form tissues and organs inside the bodies of other animals.

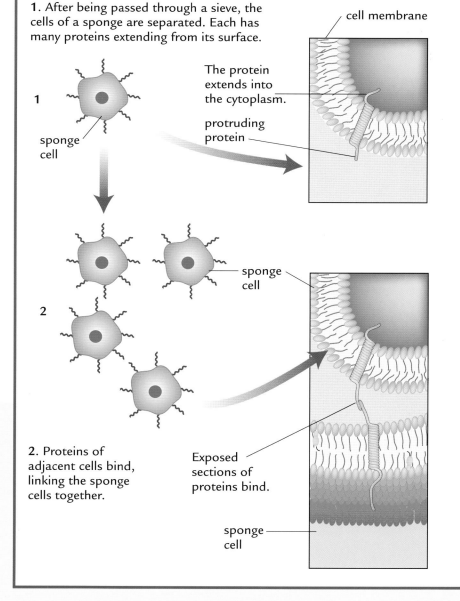

1. After being passed through a sieve, the cells of a sponge are separated. Each has many proteins extending from its surface.

cell membrane

1

sponge cell

The protein extends into the cytoplasm.

protruding protein

sponge cell

2

2. Proteins of adjacent cells bind, linking the sponge cells together.

Exposed sections of proteins bind.

sponge cell

HOW PLANT CELLS KEEP IN TOUCH

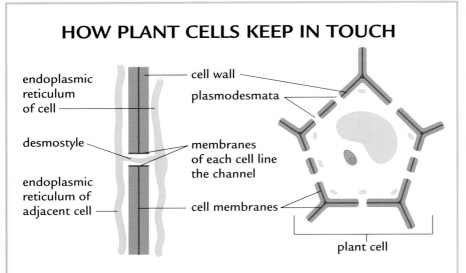

endoplasmic
reticulum
of cell

cell wall

plasmodesmata

desmostyle

membranes
of each cell line
the channel

endoplasmic
reticulum of
adjacent cell

cell membranes

plant cell

Instead of gap junctions, plants have structures called plasmodesmata. They link the cytoplasms of adjacent cells so water, ions, and small molecules can pass through easily. A tube called a desmostyle runs through each channel. This is continuous with the endoplasmic reticulum (see 33–35) of each of the adjacent cells.

Desmosomes are joints that hold cells together firmly in other parts of the body. These joints are extratough.

Desmosomes occur in places of wear and tear, such as between skin cells. But for cells to communicate, another type of junction, called a gap junction, is needed.

Gap junctions
A gap junction is a minute channel made of six protein tubes called connexons. It runs

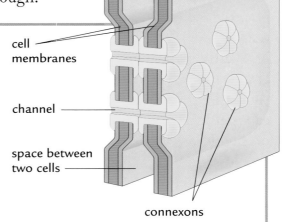

cell
membranes

channel

space between
two cells

connexons

FIGHTING HEART ATTACKS

Like other cells, heart cells contain organelles called mitochondria that produce energy. Scientists have found that heart cell death during a heart attack can be reduced by keeping open gap junctions (right) in the mitochondria. During a heart attack heart cells are deprived of oxygen and energy, so many cells die.

A junction in the mitochondria allows the movement of certain ions. By keeping these channels open, the injured heart can maintain energy and keep far more of its cells alive. Scientists are hoping to develop a molecule that will keep these gap junctions open.

The treatment could be used just after a heart attack to prevent further cell death.

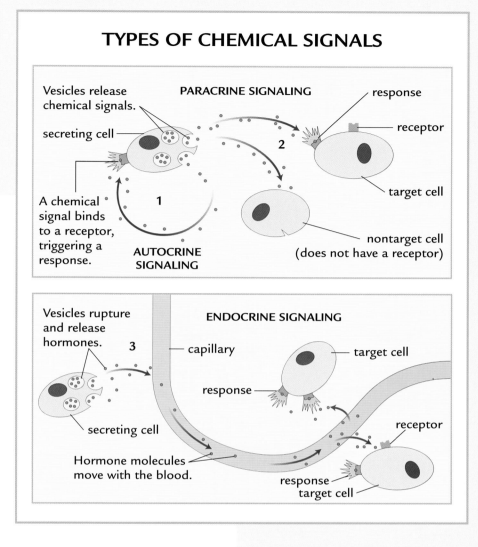

TYPES OF CHEMICAL SIGNALS

PARACRINE SIGNALING

Vesicles release chemical signals.

secreting cell

response

receptor

2

target cell

A chemical signal binds to a receptor, triggering a response.

1

nontarget cell (does not have a receptor)

AUTOCRINE SIGNALING

ENDOCRINE SIGNALING

Vesicles rupture and release hormones.

3

capillary

target cell

response

secreting cell

receptor

Hormone molecules move with the blood.

response

target cell

---

between the walls of adjacent cells. Small molecules such as salts and sugars move between neighboring cells through these channels. Gap junctions are vital for tissue function. For example, muscle cells contract in unison because electrical signals pass from one muscle cell to the next. The electrical signals are caused by the movement of particles called ions (see 49). Ions are small enough to move through gap junctions.

Gap junctions are not open doors; they do not transmit just any signal. They can change their shape, and thus the types of chemicals that can get through, depending on the needs of the cell.

Most gap junctions transmit electrical ion signals, although there are very many exceptions. Gap junctions in nonelectrically signaling tissues allow the transport of nutrients and waste in and out of cells, for example.

Chemical signals

There is a lot going on inside a cell. To ensure that everything functions as it should, different parts of a single cell need to communicate with each other. Chemicals in the cytoplasm (see 31) function as signals, telling the cell what to do. That is called intracellular signaling. Chemicals can be released and responded to by the same cell. That is called autocrine signaling.

▲ *There are three types of chemical signals. Autocrine signals (1) involve one part of the cell releasing chemicals that trigger a response in another part of the same cell. Paracrine signals (2) are targeted at nearby cells, while endocrine signals (or hormones) act over longer distances (3).*

REGULATING SUGAR LEVELS

There are many examples of the importance of communication in the body and the dangers of cutting the lines of contact. The level of glucose, a sugar, in the blood is kept under strict control and must be maintained within a very narrow range. The pancreas is an endocrine gland. It secretes hormones called insulin and glucagon that regulate blood-sugar levels. The pancreas gets feedback from the body that allows it to regulate the amounts of these hormones it releases.

If there is too much sugar in the blood, the pancreas secretes insulin, which helps cells absorb the excess. If there is too little sugar, glucagon is released. Glucagon molecules communicate with the liver, stimulating it to release glucose from storage. Many levels of cell communication are involved in maintaining blood-sugar levels. If communication between the blood and the pancreas is disrupted, as in the disease diabetes, blood-sugar levels can soon drift outside normal ranges, which can be deadly.

Cells also use chemicals to communicate with other cells over short distances. This is called paracrine signaling. Chemicals used in paracrine signaling are often produced in high concentrations.

Chemical communication between cells over longer distances in the body is called endocrine signaling. Endocrine signals are formed by hormones. They are chemicals secreted by endocrine glands (see **7**: 54–55), which include the pituitary, adrenal, and thyroid glands. The hormones are carried through the blood to the places where they are needed. Hormones are among the most common

HOW DO PAINKILLERS WORK?

Painkillers (right) block the chemicals that pass the sensation of pain through the nervous system to the brain. There are two types of painkillers. One type, including aspirin, halts the body's production of prostaglandins, chemicals that produce the sensation of pain. Other painkillers block receptors in the brain so the pain sensations cannot be received.

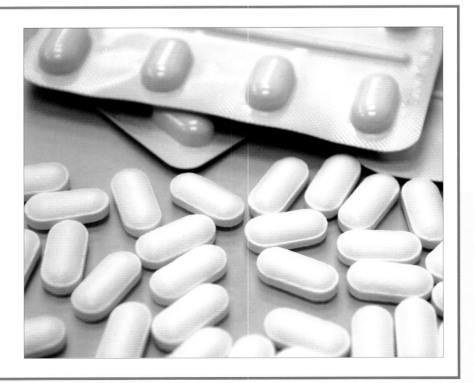

of the body's chemical signals, although each is usually produced in low concentrations.

Getting the message

All cells have receptors on their surfaces. A receptors' shape only allows it to bind with specific molecules. The molecule (such as a hormone) that binds to a receptor is its ligand. The receptors are made of proteins, which are intricately folded molecules. The number, type, and arrangement of proteins determine which of the chemical signals carried in the blood the receptor is able to receive.

The receptor–ligand system is like a lock and key: The receptor is the lock, while the ligand is the only key that can open it. When the lock is opened, the ligand can get to work on the cell. Once bound with a ligand, a cell receptor responds in one of several ways. Some receptors move into the cytoplasm with the

WHAT IS AN ION?

Electrical signals in the body depend on the movement of particles called ions. All matter is made up of tiny particles called atoms. Each atom has a nucleus orbited by one or more tiny electrons. The nucleus contains positively charged particles called protons and usually also particles called neutrons that do not have a charge. Electrons have a negative charge. In an atom the positive and negative charges balance each other out. However, an atom may lose or gain one or more electrons. It then becomes electrically charged. These charged atoms are called ions.

For example, table salt is a chemical compound called sodium chloride, or NaCl. When dissolved in water, the compound separates out, producing two types of ions. Sodium ions lose one electron, so they are positively charged (Na^+). Chloride ions hang onto the electron lost by the sodium, so they are negatively charged (Cl^-).

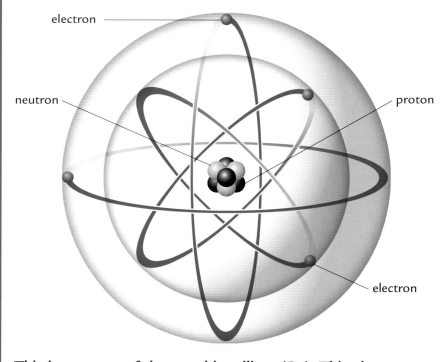

This is an atom of the metal beryllium (Be). This element forms ions by losing its two outer electrons to become Be^{2+}

APPLICATIONS

TREATING PARKINSON'S DISEASE

Parkinson's disease is caused by a deficiency of a chemical called dopamine. It is caused by the death of cells that make this substance. Amounts of another brain chemical, acetylcholine, then increase. It is this chemical that causes the tremors that characterize Parkinson's. The disease can be treated with a dopamine substitute called L-dopa. Although the drug eases the symptoms, it cannot cure the disease.

▲ *The greatest heavyweight boxer of all time, Muhammad Ali (born 1942). After his retirement from boxing in the 1980s Ali's voice began to slur, he developed uncontrollable shaking, and he had trouble with limb coordination. These problems were symptoms of Parkinson's disease, of which Ali is a sufferer.*

ligand attached. Other receptors activate molecules in the cell membrane that create new chemicals. The new chemicals carry the message into the cell. Some receptors create channels in the cell membrane through which ions can move. The movement of ions across the cell membrane alters the cell's electrical properties.

Whichever type of action takes place, the binding of ligand molecule to receptor causes a cascade of messenger chemicals to move inside the cell. These messengers carry out the tasks directed by the ligand.

Important cAMP

One of the most important messengers inside the cell is a molecule called cyclic AMP, or cAMP. Normally the concentration of this messenger in a cell is very low. But when a ligand binds to a receptor, an enzyme in the cell membrane starts churning out lots of cAMP. The cAMP moves from the cell membrane into the cytoplasm. There it activates a range of enzymes. They are proteins that help chemical reactions take place and so control the behavior of the cell. The cAMP can also trigger a cascade of chemical reactions that speed up the cell's response to the ligand.

Sometimes such chemical go-betweens are not required. In these cases the receptor–ligand complex causes parts of the cell membrane to bunch up. The bunched-up segment of membrane moves into the cell. There it fuses with certain organelles inside, activating them.

The receptors on cells triggered by insulin and other hormones are called tyrosine

HOW SYNAPSES WORK

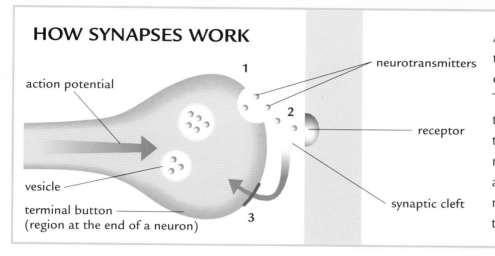

action potential

neurotransmitters

vesicle

receptor

terminal button
(region at the end of a neuron)

synaptic cleft

An action potential triggers the rupture of packets of neurotransmitters (**1**). The chemicals pass through the synaptic cleft. They bind to receptors on another neuron (**2**), causing another action potential. Spare neurotransmitters are then reabsorbed (**3**).

kinase receptors. Sometimes these receptors malfunction, and communication with the cell breaks down. Problems with tyrosine kinase receptors may lead to diseases like type II diabetes (see box on 48).

Ultimate communicators

It is not just chemicals that carry messages around the body. Cells also communicate by using electrical impulses. This forms the basis of the nervous system (see **7**: 44–55). Nerve cells, or neurons, carry impulses between your brain and every other part of your body.

Neurons are master communicators, both with each other and with the cells that form the tissues and organs of the body. All neurons contain dendrites, threadlike extensions that receive messages from other nerve cells and

transmit the messages to the neuron cell body. The cell body contains the nucleus, mitochondria, and various other organelles. The axon is a long, stringy extension of the neuron. It conducts messages from the nerve cell body to other neurons.

The messages carried by neurons are electrical. Each message is called an action potential. It is a spike of electrical activity caused by the movement of different types of ions in and out of the neuron (see **7**: 48).

Messages move between neurons across a junction called a synapse. The journey requires tiny molecules called neurotransmitters. They cross the synapse and bind to receptors on the next neuron along. That prompts a new action potential, allowing the electrical message to go on.

MULTIPLE SCLEROSIS

Myelin is a fibrous sheath that surrounds nerve cells in the brain, spinal cord, and optic nerves. Myelin also plays an important role in helping neurons transmit electrical signals around the body. Without the myelin sheath nerve cell communication is severely hampered. Multiple sclerosis (MS) is a disease in which the body's immune (self-defense) system attacks the myelin. That leads to problems with eyesight, chronic fatigue, the loss of limb coordination, and organ failure. Scientists do not know exactly what causes MS, but its interruption of signal transmission along neurons can be fatal.

6 The Cell Cycle

Most cells go through a series of life stages called the cell cycle.

DYING TO BE USEFUL

Some cells opt out of the cell cycle, but they do so at a cost—death. However, death can be an inevitable part of a cell's function. Take toenails, for example. The cells that make up your toenails and fingernails become filled with a tough, flexible protein called keratin. The keratin swiftly kills the cells, which are more useful dead than alive. The tough, dead nail cells protect the sensitive upper parts of toes and fingers from wear.

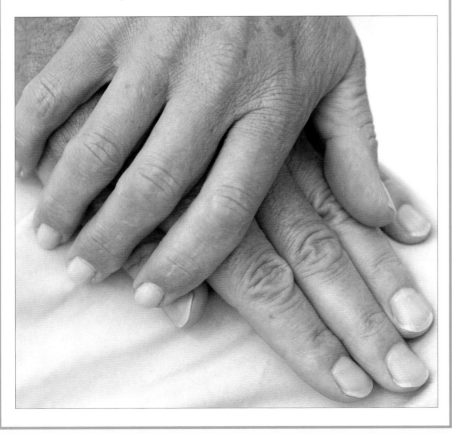

Nearly all cells, whether they are free-living single-celled organisms such as bacteria or part of the tissues of a multicellular organism, go through a series of life stages called the cell cycle. The cell cycle includes cell growth, copying of its genetic information, or DNA (see **3: 26–37**), and finally, the division of one cell into two.

Different cycles

There are two types of cells. They are called prokaryote and eukaryote cells. Prokaryotes are an ancient group of single-celled organisms that include bacteria (see **4: 8–19**). Prokaryote cells do not have nuclei (control centers; see **32–33**). Instead, their single strand of DNA floats freely within the cell cytoplasm (see **31–32**).

BENEFICIAL BINARY FISSION

Binary fission is a form of asexual reproduction (see **8**: 10–19). Genetic material is not exchanged, so bacteria have little genetic diversity. However, binary fission does allow bacteria to increase their numbers with amazing swiftness. Bacteria still shuffle their genes occasionally, through a process called conjugation (see **8**: 17).

Animals, plants, fungi, and protists (see **4**: 20–31) all consist solely of eukaryote cells. The DNA of eukaryotes is parceled up inside the nucleus. Eukaryote cells also contain miniorgans called organelles, which prokaryotes lack. Organelles include the chloroplasts (see 39) and the mitochondria (see 41–42).

When not dividing, cells function in similar ways. They take in food, convert it into energy, and manufacture proteins and other products. However, there are some distinct differences in the ways prokaryote and eukaryote cells divide in two.

Binary fission

Prokaryote cell division is called binary fission. Before the cell divides, its single DNA strand replicates, or self-copies (see **3**: 29–31). The two DNA copies attach to the inside of the cell membrane. The membrane begins to stretch. As it elongates, the DNA strands are pulled apart. Soon the cell is so stretched that it has effectively doubled its size. Then

▼ *These are diatoms, plantlike organisms that float among the plankton near the surface of the ocean. Binary fission of one diatom into two has just come to an end.*

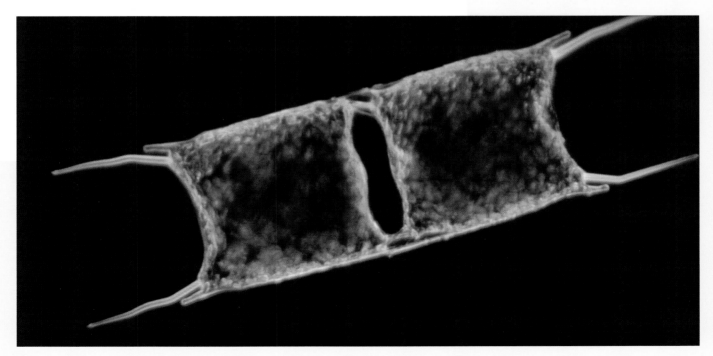

APPLICATIONS

CELLS THAT HELP IVF

Cells in a culture can move through their cell cycles very quickly. Medical researchers exploit this to produce drugs. They implant genes (see **3**: 34) that produce drugs into cells. The cells increase in number until the drug can be harvested.

Couples that struggle to have children sometimes have *in vitro* fertilization (IVF) treatment. Eggs are fertilized with sperm outside the body. The fertilized eggs are then placed in the woman's uterus. To make the woman's ovary release the extra eggs needed,

a hormone, FSH, is required. FSH was once drawn from the urine of women going through menopause (see **8**: 69). Today, human genes that code for FSH are implanted into cells from the ovary of a Chinese hamster. The cells are cultured, and the hormone is collected. This process produces larger quantities of FSH than existing techniques and also eliminates the possibility of infection.

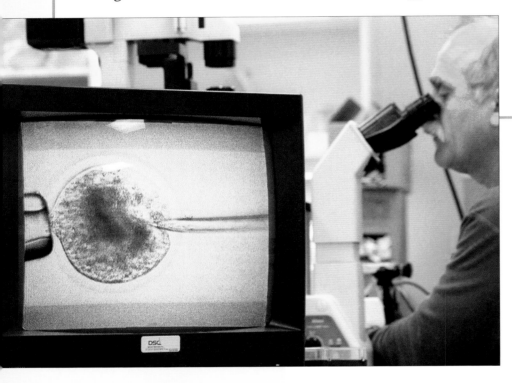

▲ In vitro *fertilization in action. The physician is carefully injecting sperm into an egg. The egg was collected from the woman undergoing treatment after she had been injected with FSH hormone.*

the cell membrane begins to pinch inward at the center of the long, elongated cell. The cell's "waist" gets smaller and smaller as the membrane pinches inward. Eventually the two parts of the membrane meet in the middle of the cell.

Once the cell is completely pinched in two, a new cell wall forms in its center. The two new (or daughter) cells then split apart. The cells are genetically identical. One has the original DNA from the parent cell, while the other has an exact copy.

The eukaryote cell cycle

Nearly all eukaryote cells go through the same stages, or phases, during their cell cycle. There are four phases, each designated by a letter. They are the G1 phase, S phase, G2 phase, and M phase. The G stands for gap, the S stands for synthesis, and the M stands for mitosis.

DECEPTIVE SLUMBER

In the nineteenth century biologists only had light microscopes to observe cells. They could see absolutely nothing of interest going on inside a cell during interphase. So interphase was dubbed the cells' resting phase. Biologists now know that a cell gets no rest at all during this time. Through electron microscopy (see **1**: 50–51) biologists have shown that the cell seethes with activity during interphase. DNA replicates in the nucleus, while the organelles work in a frenzy, producing proteins and other products as well as liberating energy from food.

Understanding interphase

Phases G1, S, and G2 are together known as interphase. During interphase the cell uses energy to perform functions like the production of proteins (see **3**: 26–37). At the end of interphase chemical signals within the cell prepare it for cell division (see 58). The DNA of the cell must replicate, and a supply of organelles for the daughter cells must also be produced.

During the first gap phase, or G1, the cell increases the amount of cytoplasm it contains. It doubles in size and builds many of the extra organelles. G1 is usually the longest phase in the cell cycle. Chemicals determine how long G1 lasts (see 58). When the cell stops growing, G1 comes to a halt. More chemicals then launch the cell into the next stage, the S phase.

The S, or synthesis, phase involves the replication of the cell's DNA inside the

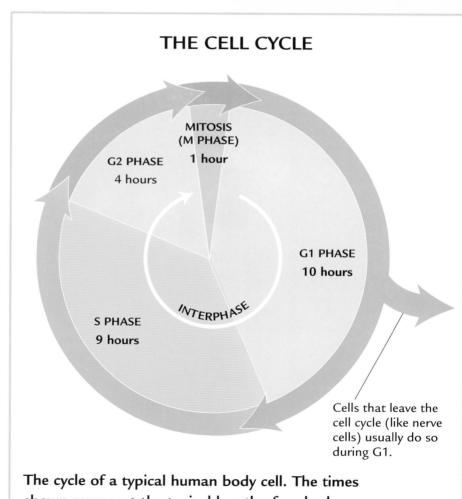

THE CELL CYCLE

MITOSIS (M PHASE) 1 hour

G2 PHASE 4 hours

G1 PHASE 10 hours

S PHASE 9 hours

INTERPHASE

Cells that leave the cell cycle (like nerve cells) usually do so during G1.

The cycle of a typical human body cell. The times shown represent the typical length of each phase.

G1 AND CANCER RESEARCH

APPLICATIONS

Medical researchers are looking for chemicals that end the cell cycle prematurely during the G1 phase. These substances might help in the war against cancer. Cancer cells grow and divide uncontrollably (see 62–70). Cells might become cancerous because of an error in the G1 chemical mechanism that controls cell growth and division. It normally stops any further cell growth. More research is required, but these control substances may one day offer a cure for a range of cancers.

During G2 the cell begins to put together all the structures it will need to separate its genetic material, allowing it to produce two daughter cells.

Mitosis

G2 is followed by mitosis, or the M phase. Mitosis allows tissues to grow or repair by creating new cells. Mitosis involves the separation of genetic material into two new sets (see **3**: 18–20).

▼ *This boy has broken his arm. Healing depends on mitosis. Cells divide to fix the break. Mitosis ensures that the cells contain DNA that is identical to all other body cells.*

nucleus. The proteins needed by the cell for division are also created during this phase.

Once DNA replication is complete, the cell moves into the second gap phase, G2.

Each new cell formed through mitosis needs a complete set of the organism's DNA; it must be as similar as possible to the DNA of every other body cell.

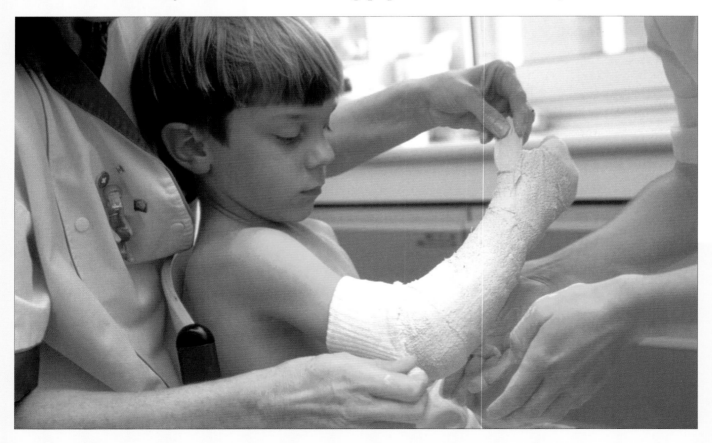

Mitosis is itself divided into four phases. The first is called prophase. During prophase DNA in the nucleus coils up with proteins to form structures called chromatids. Pairs of sister (identical) chromatids link at their midpoints to form chromosomes.

Meanwhile, tiny structures called centrioles begin to assemble outside the nucleus. The centrioles move to opposite ends of the cell, and a network of fibers called the spindle (see 24) grows between them. The membrane of the nucleus then begins to break down.

Metaphase to telophase

Next, in the phase called metaphase the chromosomes line up at the center of the cell, or equator. There they rest on the spindle.

The next stage, anaphase, sees the cell's chromosomes wrenched apart by the spindle fibers. The chromatids from

▶ *The stages of mitotic cell division. Note that this diagram shows division in an animal cell. Things go in a similar way in plants, but cytokinesis is different (see 59).*

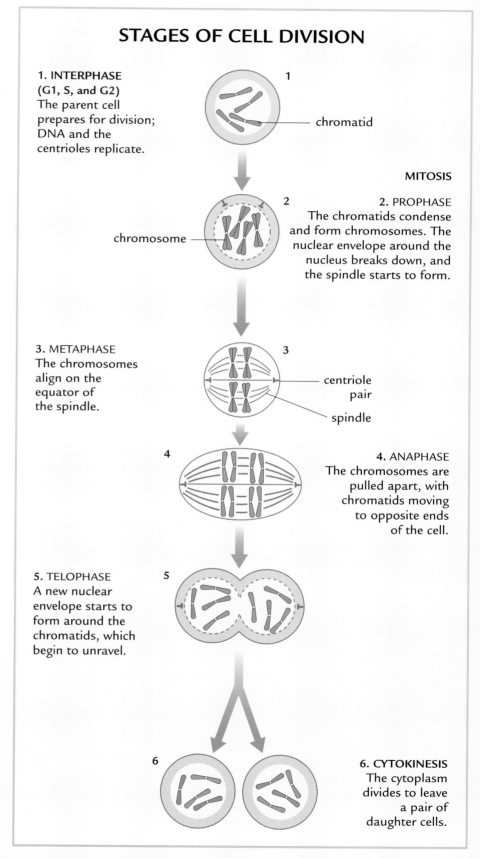

STAGES OF CELL DIVISION

1. INTERPHASE (G1, S, and G2) The parent cell prepares for division; DNA and the centrioles replicate.

chromatid

MITOSIS

chromosome

2. PROPHASE The chromatids condense and form chromosomes. The nuclear envelope around the nucleus breaks down, and the spindle starts to form.

3. METAPHASE The chromosomes align on the equator of the spindle.

centriole pair

spindle

4. ANAPHASE The chromosomes are pulled apart, with chromatids moving to opposite ends of the cell.

5. TELOPHASE A new nuclear envelope starts to form around the chromatids, which begin to unravel.

6. CYTOKINESIS The cytoplasm divides to leave a pair of daughter cells.

CONTROLLING THE CELL CYCLE

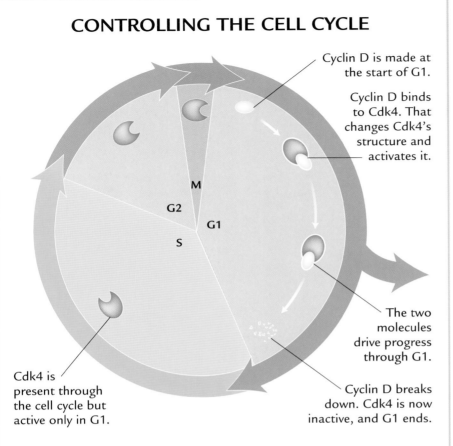

Cyclin D is made at the start of G1.

Cyclin D binds to Cdk4. That changes Cdk4's structure and activates it.

The two molecules drive progress through G1.

Cyclin D breaks down. Cdk4 is now inactive, and G1 ends.

Cdk4 is present through the cell cycle but active only in G1.

Different Cdk and cyclin molecules are important at different points of the cell cycle: Cdk2–cyclin E acts at the start of the S phase; Cdk2–cyclin A acts during the S phase; and Cdk1–cyclin B acts at the G2-M boundary.

◀ *The cell cycle is regulated by a protein called Cdk (see 3: 17). It binds to another chemical called cyclin to trigger a new phase. Different types of Cdk and cyclin control different parts of the cell cycle.*

each of the pairs move in opposite directions toward the ends of the cell.

During this final stage of mitosis the spindle begins to disintegrate. The chromatids (or daughter chromosomes, as they are now known) begin to unravel. A new nuclear membrane begins to form around each set of chromosomes.

One becomes two

Mitosis serves only to separate the two copies of the cell's DNA. Once this has been accomplished, the cell itself must physically divide. Biologists call this process cytokinesis. It involves the division of the cell cytoplasm into two. Animal and plant cytokinesis takes place in different ways.

Animal cells divide by first forming a dent along the cell equator. This is called the equatorial furrow. Tiny fibers in the cytoplasm make the cell membrane pinch inward,

OBSERVING CHROMOSOMES

German biologist Walther Flemming (1843–1905) perfected observation techniques for cells. Flemming fixed cells at various stages of their life cycle. Then he stained them so he could observe the parts inside. Using dyes, Flemming could watch the chromosomes that became visible during cell division. His techniques were so efficient that he was able to see how the chromosomes divided between the daughter cells. Flemming named the division of body cells mitosis, from a Greek word meaning "thread." This referred to the threadlike appearance of chromosomes.

forming a waist in the center of the cell. The furrow quickly deepens into a groove and carries on constricting until the cell cleaves in two. Finally, a new cell membrane forms, separating the two daughter cells.

Plant division

Plants cells have rigid walls, so they are not easily pinched inward. During telophase in plants dense material collects on a structure called a phragmoplast (see box). It forms a double plate along the cell equator. The double plate grows until the cell is completely divided into two cells. When cell division is complete, each daughter cell has a fully formed cell wall at the site of the equator.

In both animals and plants the cell cycle begins again once cytokinesis is complete. The cell goes through the three stages of interphase until it is again time to divide.

PHRAGMOPLASTS

To successfully divide, a plant cell needs a structure called a phragmoplast. A phragmoplast is a series of fibers that forms along the midline between dividing cells. Packages (or vesicles) containing cellulose for building new cell walls are carried by proteins to the phragmoplast. They travel along the spindle fibers formed during mitosis. At the phragmoplast the packages rupture. The cellulose is then arranged by the fibers.

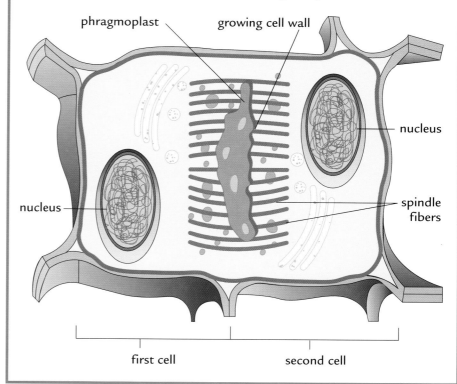

Strange stem cells

Not all cells follow this typical life cycle. Nerve cells (see box on page 61) and fingernail cells (see box on page 52) buck the trend. So do red blood cells. They do not have nuclei, so they cannot divide. Red blood cells are produced

Vast numbers of red blood cells are produced from stem cells—around 2.5 million each second! Red blood cells do not have nuclei, so they cannot divide. After a few months they are broken down inside the spleen. The cells contain a pigment called hemoglobin that allows them to carry oxygen around the body.

by blood stem cells. They are cells in the bone marrow whose sole purpose is to create new blood cells.

Blood stem cells reproduce extremely rapidly because red blood cells must be replaced constantly. Yet the destiny of a cell produced by blood stem cells is not predetermined. Many develop into red blood cells. But other daughter cells become white blood cells (see **7**: 66–70), while the rest divide again and again to produce more blood stem cells.

Division in sex cells

Like blood cells, sex cells (sperm and eggs) do not go through an endless cycle of growth followed by division. In organisms that reproduce sexually (see **8**: 20–31), the sex cells contain half the normal number of chromosomes (see **3**: 20–21). Sex cells are produced by sex stem cells that occur in the testes (in males) or ovaries (in females). The process of division that leads to sex cells is called meiosis (see **3**: 20–25).

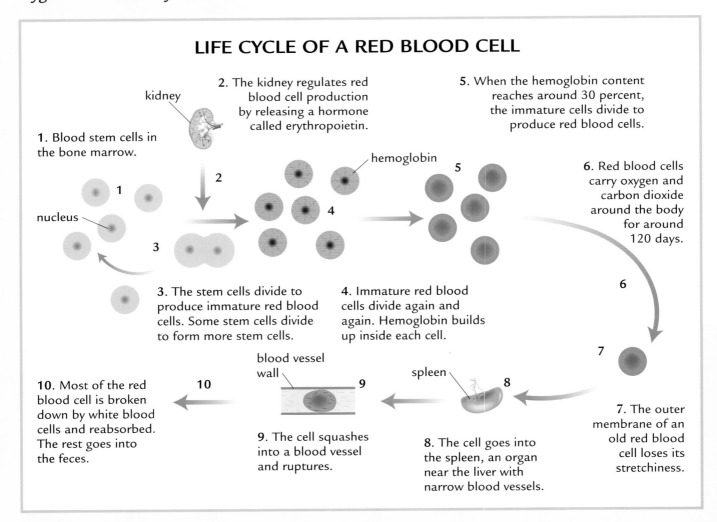

LIFE CYCLE OF A RED BLOOD CELL

1. Blood stem cells in the bone marrow.

nucleus

2. The kidney regulates red blood cell production by releasing a hormone called erythropoietin.

kidney

hemoglobin

3. The stem cells divide to produce immature red blood cells. Some stem cells divide to form more stem cells.

4. Immature red blood cells divide again and again. Hemoglobin builds up inside each cell.

5. When the hemoglobin content reaches around 30 percent, the immature cells divide to produce red blood cells.

6. Red blood cells carry oxygen and carbon dioxide around the body for around 120 days.

7. The outer membrane of an old red blood cell loses its stretchiness.

8. The cell goes into the spleen, an organ near the liver with narrow blood vessels.

spleen

blood vessel wall

9. The cell squashes into a blood vessel and ruptures.

10. Most of the red blood cell is broken down by white blood cells and reabsorbed. The rest goes into the feces.

Meiosis is similar to mitosis in some ways, but its aim is very different. Mitosis leads to cells that are genetically identical to their parents. Meiosis produces sex cells that are genetically distinct from the parent stem cells. Sex cells cannot divide. A few unite with sex cells from mates to produce young. All the other sex cells die.

APPLICATIONS

CELLS FOR LIFE

Your body contains some cells that will stay alive without dividing for the rest of your life. Some of these cells developed when you were an embryo in your mother's uterus. Nerve cells are among these unchanging cells. When nerve cells are damaged through injury, it is extremely difficult to regrow them because such cells do not normally divide. Medical researchers are looking for ways to trick nerve cells into dividing so damaged nerves can heal. The researchers hunt for chemicals that will trigger cell division or study how stem cells work. Such research may one day allow people paralyzed by spinal cord injuries, for example, to live normal lives.

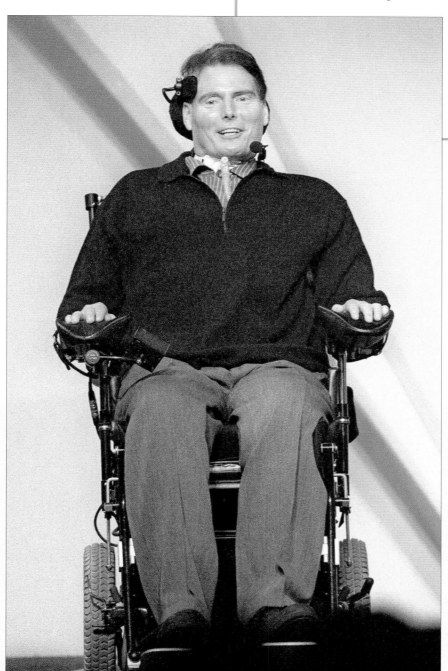

◀ *The movie actor Christopher Reeve (born 1952) was paralyzed from the neck down in a 1995 horse-riding accident. Stem cell research may one day allow Reeve and others like him to walk again.*

Cells Out Of Control

Cells sometimes reproduce and grow abnormally, resulting in diseases such as cancer.

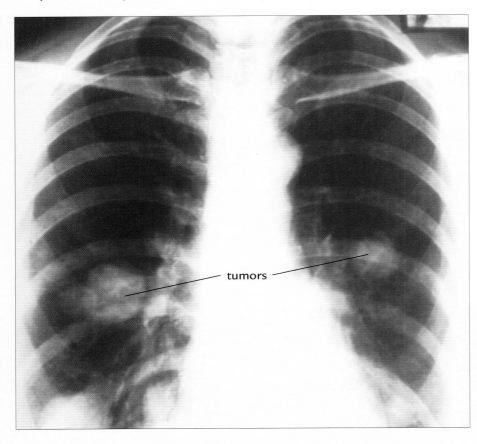

▼ *A chest x-ray reveals so-called "cannonball" cancerous tumors in the patient's lungs.*

tumors

Since you were born, your body has grown steadily and in a controlled way. You never found that your left arm had grown much longer than your right, or that your right foot had become six shoe sizes bigger than your left foot. Your arms and legs elongate at the same time and at the same rate. The genetic (inherited) information in the cells of your body ensures that your growth is properly timed and controlled.

Your body's cells also develop, reproduce, and die in a controlled way (see 52–61). Sometimes, however, the genetic mechanisms that regulate cell behavior fail. Then cells may grow uncontrollably, and the disease called cancer might develop. Cancer occurs when a mass, or tumor, develops from a single cell growing out of control.

Genes and control
Genes are codes that regulate the making of proteins. Many of these proteins do the work

MANY FROM ONE

In the 1850s German biologist Rudolf Virchow (1821–1902) developed his single-cell theory of tumors. He stated that all the cells in a tumor originated from a single cancerous cell. As that cell divides, it creates cancerous copies of itself. Virchow was correct, and his theory still underlies research into cancer as a disease of cells.

in a cell (see **3**: 31–36). To regulate cell growth, proteins either initiate (start) or inhibit (stop) cell division. Proto-oncogenes code for proteins that switch cell division on, while tumor-suppressor genes code for proteins that switch cell division off. Cancer may develop when a mutation (change or fault) occurs in either of these types of genes.

A mutation in a proto-oncogene (see 66) might cause a cell to divide endlessly, forming a tumor. A tumor-suppressor gene (see 66) may be disabled by a mutation, so cell division is not ended but continues indefinitely, producing a tumor. Genes that cause cancer are called oncogenes.

Genetic mutations (see **9**: 26–31) happen all the time. But every cell has the ability to repair damaged or mutated genes. Most of the time this repair mechanism works well. If the genetic damage is massive, a cell can even commit suicide. Cell suicide, or apoptosis (see below and 67) prevents damaged cells from reproducing. It is only when cell repair or apoptosis fails that mutations may cause cell division to spin out of control.

CAUSES OF MUTATIONS

Sometimes the offspring of a sexually reproducing animal

DIVIDING CELLS

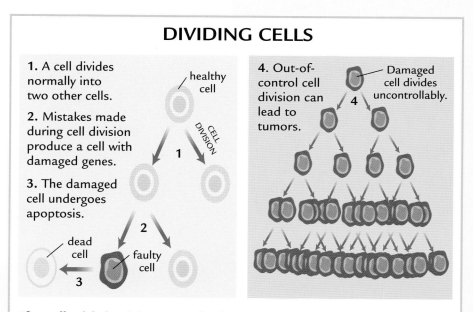

1. A cell divides normally into two other cells.

2. Mistakes made during cell division produce a cell with damaged genes.

3. The damaged cell undergoes apoptosis.

healthy cell

CELL DIVISION

dead cell

faulty cell

4. Out-of-control cell division can lead to tumors.

Damaged cell divides uncontrollably.

If a cell with healthy genes is damaged, the cell either repairs itself or undergoes apoptosis (cell suicide; 1–3). If the genes that control cell division fail, however, cells divide uncontrollably (4).

WHAT DO YOU THINK?

RISING INCIDENCE

Since 1973 the incidence of many types of cancers has increased dramatically. For example, there has been about a doubling of rates of testicular cancer (from 3.3 to 5.8 per 100,000) and prostate cancer (from 80 to 175 per 100,000). Breast cancer rates have increased from 100 to 138 per 100,000; melanoma (a deadly skin cancer) from 7.6 to 26 per 100,000.

The testes and the prostate are organs of the male reproductive system (see **8**: 44). Some scientists blame the increase in reproductive cancers on artificial hormone-mimicking chemicals in the environment (see **8**: 52). Yet few governments, businesses, or individuals seem to be taking action to reverse these trends by trying to eliminate possible cancer-causing agents from the environment.

Other factors can also cause the increase in rates of cancer. For example, people live longer due to improved medical care and are more likely to get cancer as they age. What do you think are the main causes?

The map shows the percentage of deaths due to cancer in different areas of the world. In 2000 more than 6.2 million people died from cancer.

| <5% | 5–10% | 10–15% | 15–20% | 20–25% | >25% |

inherits a mutated gene from one or both parents, and that gene may lead to cancer. A mutation in the *RB* gene, for example, causes an inherited form of eye cancer called retinoblastoma in children. Normally *RB* is bound to and controls a protein, E2F, that starts cell division. If the *RB* gene mutates, E2F is neither bound nor regulated, so it causes uncontrolled division of eye cells, leading to cancer.

Viral oncogenes

In 1968 researchers studying a virus (see **4**: 32–43) discovered that when it inserts its genes into a cell, the genes in the cell are mutated, and the cell becomes cancerous. This viral gene was called *src*, the first oncogene identified.

Human papilloma virus (HPV) might cause cancer of the cervix (the "neck" of the uterus; see **8**: 55). The virus hepatitis B might cause liver cancer. These viruses force infected cells to reproduce wildly. In the course of this reproductive frenzy infected cells can undergo genetic mutations that eventually lead to cancerous tumors.

MUMMIFIED CANCERS

Although cancer is often thought of as a modern disease, it did afflict ancient peoples. Scientists have found 5,000-year-old mummies in Egypt and Peru whose skeletons show definite signs that these individuals suffered from cancer.

Chemical and environmental causes

Chemicals used to make plastics, such as vinyl chloride, are known to cause mutations that cause liver cancer. Many genes help control cell division, thereby preventing cancer. However, different environmental factors can damage genes that control cell division. Damage of just a single gene rarely leads to cancer, because there are other genes to serve as "back-up." Damage of several key genes, by chemicals, foods, radiation, and other factors, can allow cancer to occur.

Ultraviolet (UV) radiation from the sun is increasing due to destruction of the atmospheric ozone layer (see **10: 23**). This radiation causes genetic mutations in skin cells and has led to a near epidemic of skin cancer (melanoma) in many parts of the world. Exposure to arsenic, coal, and tar can also cause melanoma.

▼ *People sunbathing on a beach may not be aware of the dangers. Skin cancer can develop unless sunbathers take precautions. They should wear hats and T-shirts, avoid being in the sun during the hottest hours of the day, and use effective sunscreens to block out harmful radiation from the sun.*

PAP SMEARS

Early detection of cancer can save lives. A pap smear is a simple, painless test named after its developer, Dr. George Papanicolaou (1883–1962). Pap smears can detect cervical cancer during its earliest stages. Because many women have pap smears every year or two, deaths from cervical cancer have decreased in recent years.

SWITCHING ERRORS

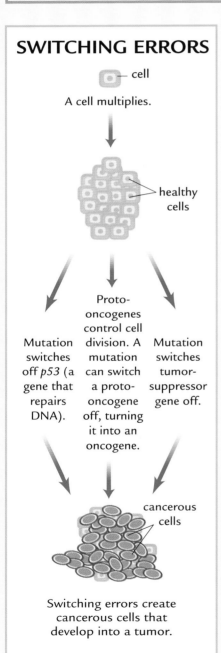

cell

A cell multiplies.

healthy cells

Proto-oncogenes control cell division. A mutation can switch a proto-oncogene off, turning it into an oncogene.

Mutation switches off *p53* (a gene that repairs DNA).

Mutation switches tumor-suppressor gene off.

cancerous cells

Switching errors create cancerous cells that develop into a tumor.

◄ *Cancer is generally a multistep process in which a series of mutations (changes) results in the production of cancerous cells. Key stages are those that affect the ability to regulate cell division.*

SWITCHING ERRORS

Mutations alter a gene's ability to send the signals that control cell functions (see 52–53). Mutations can turn normally signaling genes into oncogenes. When that happens, the normally signaling gene is said to have been "switched off" and the oncogene to be "switched on."

A normal proto-oncogene works throughout the cell cycle (see 52–61), controlling the timing of each stage of a cell's life. Proto-oncogenes control cell division by a cascade of signals that tell the cell when to produce the proteins needed for cell division. Similarly, tumor-suppressor genes stop cancerous cell division through a series of genetic signals. An unfixed mutation in one of these genes during any part of the cell-signaling cascade can disrupt cell division, and cancer may result.

Tumor-suppressor genes

The role of tumor-suppressor genes is not to suppress tumors but to inhibit or stop cell division. Yet when functioning properly, these genes suppress tumor growth by stopping cell division.

One of the best-studied tumor-suppressor genes is called *p53*. *p53* occurs in the cell's nucleus, where it monitors deoxyribonucleic acid damage. Segments of deoxyribonucleic acid, or DNA (see 3: 26–27), form genes. Slight DNA damage causes *p53* to trigger the cell's repair mechanisms. If there is severe damage, *p53* initiates apoptosis, or cell suicide (see box, right). The *p53* gene may itself suffer mutations that switch the gene off. Cells with a damaged *p53* gene cannot repair their DNA nor self-destruct. *p53* mutations are present in 70 percent of colon cancers and up to 50 percent of breast and lung cancers.

p53 is not the only gene that controls apoptosis. A mutation in the proto-oncogene *bcl-2* causes it to produce excessive quantities of a protein that blocks apoptosis. Another mutation turns on this protein permanently, so cell suicide becomes impossible.

HOW CANCER SPREADS

A cancer that grows in a vital organ can be fatal if it destroys that organ. Cancer can be fatal even if it originates in a nonvital organ because cancer can spread, or metastasize, through the body. To spread, the cells in a cancerous, or malignant, tumor

▶ *Apoptosis, or cell suicide, is triggered by a group of genes called tumor-suppressor genes.* p53 *is the tumor-suppressor gene that causes a cell with massive genetic damage to destroy itself.*

must accomplish some formidable tasks. First, they must break away from other cells; second, they must break through surrounding membranes and tissues; and third, they must find, enter, and travel through blood vessels.

All cells are embedded in the jellylike extracellular matrix. This matrix contains cell adhesion molecules, or CAMs (see 44–45), which hold cells together. When a cancer cell loses its CAMs, it is freed from other tumor cells and from the extracellular

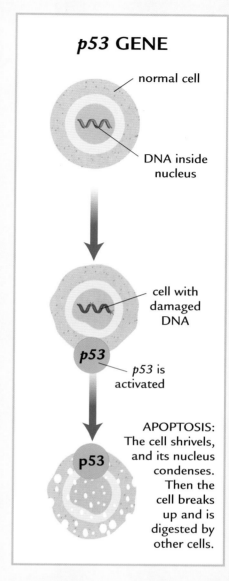

p53 GENE

normal cell

DNA inside nucleus

cell with damaged DNA

p53

p53 is activated

APOPTOSIS: The cell shrivels, and its nucleus condenses. Then the cell breaks up and is digested by other cells.

HOT DEBATE

DIET BRAIN TUMORS

Since 1973 the incidence of brain cancer has been increasing at an overall rate of about 0.7 percent annually. Researchers have linked this increase to the artificial sweetener aspartame, which is widely used in diet foods and beverages. The researchers have been pressuring the U.S. Food and Drug Administration (FDA) to ban the use of aspartame, but so far the agency has refused.

Some researchers believe that the FDA's refusal arises from its close ties to the food industry. There may be other causes of increasing brain cancer, such as radiation from electronic devices.

GENE THERAPY

Gene therapy (see **3**: 68–70) addresses the genetic mutations that lead to cancer. Scientists plan to use recombinant DNA technology (see **3**: 63) to replace a defective, mutated gene with its normal, healthy counterpart. The healthy gene is then inserted into cancer cells to restore the normal control of their reproduction.

matrix. Then the cancer cell produces enzymes that help it break through the membranes and tissues that block its path to the bloodstream.

Cancer cells invade tissues and organs by migrating into them directly. Cancers spread when cancer cells enter the bloodstream and are carried to distant organs, in which they then reproduce (see 67). The first tumor is called the primary cancer; if cancerous cells metastasize to elsewhere, those tumors are called secondary cancers.

Building blood vessels

Angiogenesis is the formation of blood vessels in a tumor. It is the stage when a tumor turns from a mass of cells into a malignant growth. Cancer cells make proteins that help build blood vessels, in particular, vascular endothelial growth factor, or VEGF. This protein attracts endothelial (lining) cells into the tumor. Endothelial cells build blood vessels. Inside the tumor they create capillaries (see **7**: 23), which bring vital nutrients and oxygen to the tumor. So VEGF enables cancer cells to build their own highway out of the tumor and into the circulatory system (see **7**: 18–25).

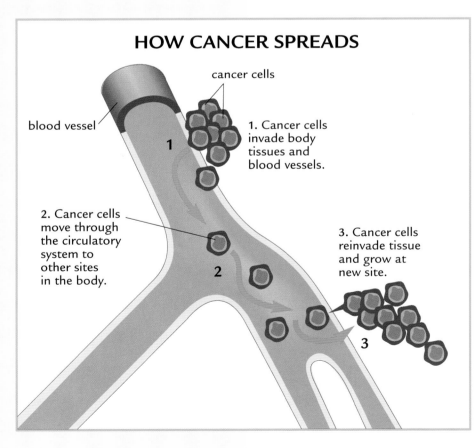

HOW CANCER SPREADS

cancer cells

blood vessel

1. Cancer cells invade body tissues and blood vessels.

2. Cancer cells move through the circulatory system to other sites in the body.

3. Cancer cells reinvade tissue and grow at new site.

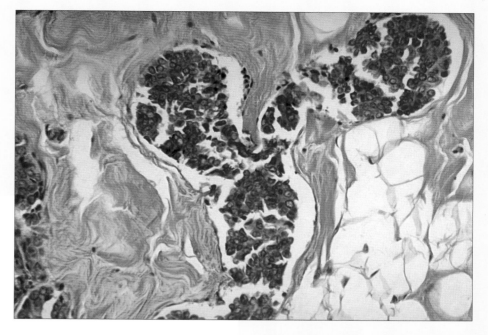

Metastasis

Scientists do not fully understand how and why different primary cancers metastasize to some organs and not others. Some cancer cells are carried around the body by the blood. After the blood has left most organs, it is pumped to the lungs by the heart. So the lungs are often the first site of metastatic cancer.

Researchers have found that some cancer cells have an attraction for cells in other parts of the body. For example, cells from breast and prostate cancer often metastasize first to bones. Scientists think that in these organs there is an attraction between receptor proteins on the surface of cancer cells and molecules in the extracellular matrix, which fills spaces among cells.

CANCER TREATMENTS

Surgery is used together with treatments such as radiotherapy and chemotherapy.

Surgery

Cutting a cancerous tumor out of the body is the most direct way of ridding the body of a malignant tumor. Until recently surgery was the only method of cancer treatment.

Surgery can be problematic because it is never certain that all the malignant cells have been removed. Physicians estimate that in two-thirds of the patients undergoing cancer surgery the cancer has already spread beyond the surgical site.

Radiotherapy

Bombarding cancer cells with radiation destroys them in one of two ways: Either the cells are so damaged they cannot reproduce, or the radiation damage causes apoptosis.

▲ *The dark purple cells in this image are breast cancer cells, magnified 30 times. Breast cancer is one of the most common cancers affecting women. Prolonged exposure to the hormone estrogen is a likely cause. This can result from an early puberty or a late menopause. Obesity may also be responsible, since excess fat causes extra estrogen to be produced. Treatment for breast cancer may involve surgery, chemotherapy, and radiotherapy.*

APPLICATIONS
CANCER PREVENTION

Cancer is not inevitable. People can avoid behaviors that are known to make them susceptible to cancer. For example, you can choose not to use tobacco, not to eat much red and fatty meat, and not to use household or garden products containing known cancer-causing agents. To reduce the risk of getting skin cancer, avoid going out in strong sun. When outdoors, always wear a hat and light clothing, and use an effective sunscreen.

There are two types of radiation treatment. In internal radiotherapy a radioactive material is inserted into the body near the tumor. External radiotherapy is when a beam of radiation is directed at the site of the tumor from an apparatus outside the body. The radiation is administered in tiny pulses that minimize complications and side effects.

Chemotherapy

Chemotherapy uses drugs to kill cancer cells. Most of these chemicals prevent cancer cells from multiplying. One advantage of chemotherapy is that the chemicals travel throughout the body and can kill cancer cells almost anywhere they are found. Most chemotherapy patients suffer side effects such as vomiting and hair loss because the chemicals often kill healthy cells as well as cancerous ones.

Cutting-edge treatments

Today physicians use their greater understanding of how cancer cells function to fight the disease. One new treatment is called angiogenesis inhibition. It involves giving the patient drugs to prevent angiogenesis (see 68).

Immunotherapy uses the body's own immune system to fight the cancer. The immune system's B-cells (see **7**: 25) recognize particles called antigens on the surface of foreign cells and build proteins called antibodies (see **7**: 69–70) to destroy the cells. (Antigens are anything that provoke an immune system response.)

Researchers have also identified antigens on the surfaces of cancer cells. Now scientists are finding ways to create antibodies that kill tumor cells. Another recent approach involves using vaccines (see **4**: 49–51) to stimulate the body's own immune system to attack and kill cancer cells.

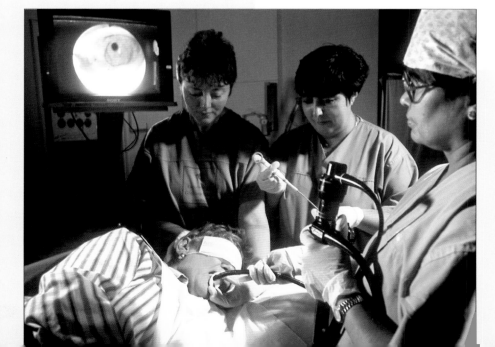

◀ *Physicians perform an endoscopy. An endoscope is a fiber-optic cable with a tiny camera at one end. It produces an image on a screen. The physicians remove a sample of tissue (biopsy) from the stomach and use it to diagnose cancer.*

More Information

Books

Coopersmith Gold, J. *Cancer.* Berkeley Heights, NJ: Enslow Publishers, 2001.

Ganeri, A. *Life Processes: Cells and Systems.* Chicago, IL: Heinemann Library, 2002.

Llamas Ruiz, A. *The Life of a Cell.* New York: Sterling Publishers, 1998.

Parker, S. *Body Focus: Spinal Cord and Nerves: Injury, Illness, and Health.* Chicago, IL: Heinemann Library, 2003.

Sharth, S. *Sea Jellies: From Corals to Jellyfish.* New York: Franklin Watts, Inc., 2002.

Silverstein, A., Silverstein, V. B., and Silverstein Nunn, L. *Parkinson's Disease.* Berkeley Heights, NJ: Enslow Publishers, 2002.

Sneddon, R. *The Diversity of Life: From Single Cells to Multicellular Organisms.* Chicago, IL: Heinemann Library, 2002.

Spilsbury, R and Spilsbury, L. *Plant Parts.* Chicago, IL: Heinemann Library, 2003.

Tesar, J. *Science on the Edge: Stem Cells.* San Diego, CA: Blackbirch Press, 2003.

Websites

Animal Cell Diagram
www.syvum.com/cgi/online/serve.cgi/squizzes/biology/animalcell.tdf
Label the parts of an animal cell, and click to find out if you were correct.

Cells Alive!
www.cellsalive.com/index.htm
Loads of information and visuals about cells, including animations and videos, microphotographs, and illustrations of cells and organelles.

Cells Are Us
peer.tamu.edu/curriculum_modules/Cell_Biology/
Middle-school instruction on cell biology from the Texas A&M University.

Cells R Us
www.icnet.uk/kids/cellsrus/cellsrus.html
The Imperial Cancer Research Fund's online slide show about cells.

How Cells Work
science.howstuffworks.com/cell.htm
Text and graphics that provide a sound introduction to cell biology.

MicroAngela Cells
www.pbrc.hawaii.edu/bemf/microangela/cells.htm
Browse false-color photos of cells taken with a scanning electron microscope at the University of Hawaii.

The Virtual Cell
www.ibiblio.org/virtualcell/index.htm
Use a virtual textbook, print out worksheets, or take The Virtual Cell Tour, on which you can rotate and zoom in on organelles.

Virtual Plant Cell
www.life.uiuc.edu/plantbio/cell/
An interactive journey through a plant cell. Read "About Virtual Cell" to understand the controls.

Glossary

angiogenesis The formation of blood vessels by cancer tumors.

antigen Molecule (often on the surface of a foreign body) that the immune system can recognize.

apoptosis Cell suicide triggered by tumor-suppressor genes.

autocrine signaling When a cell sends out chemical signals but receives and acts on them itself.

axon Long extension of a neuron that carries electrical signals.

cell adhesion molecule (CAM) Molecule that allows a cell to stick only to similar cells.

cell cycle Life cycle of a cell.

centriole Structure in the cell that helps form the spindle.

chloroplast Organelle that carries out photosynthesis.

chromosome Structure that forms during cell division and is made of DNA.

cilium Small filament that occurs in banks on the surface of many cells.

cyclic AMP (cAMP) Messenger chemical that drives a cell's response to a hormone.

cytologist Biologist who studies cells.

cytokinesis The physical separation of one cell into two after meiosis or mitosis.

cytoplasm Region of a cell outside the nucleus.

cytoskeleton Fibers in the cytoplasm that provide a cell with structural support.

cytosol Liquid that forms much of the cytoplasm.

desmosome Tough joint that holds cells together.

deoxyribonucleic acid (DNA) Molecule that contains the genetic code for all cellular (nonvirus) organisms.

dynein Protein that allows cilia and flagella to move.

egg Female sex cell.

endocrine signaling Long-distance signaling using hormones.

endocytosis When a cell takes in molecules or particles.

enzyme Protein that speeds up chemical reactions inside an organism.

eukaryote cell Cell of a plant, animal, fungus, or protist; contains structures called organelles.

exocytosis The process cells use to get rid of substances.

flagellum Long, tail-like structure used for locomotion by many single-celled organisms.

gap junction Tiny channel connecting two cells through which small molecules can pass.

genome All the genes present inside an organism.

Golgi apparatus Organelle that alters and packages molecules made in other parts of the cell.

Haversian canal Channel through which blood vessels bring nutrients to bone cells.

hormone Chemical messenger that regulates life processes inside the body.

hydrophilic Molecule that repels water.

hydrophobic Molecule that attracts water.

interphase Nondividing part of a cell's life cycle.

lysosome Organelle that breaks down large molecules, such as proteins.

meiosis Process of cell division that leads to sex cell production.

metastasis The movement of cancer cells from one part of the body to another.

mitochondrion Organelle that produces energy from food and oxygen.

mitosis Process of cell division that leads to the production of body cells.

mutation A change in a cell's DNA.

myelin sheath Fatty coating of a neuron.

nanometer One twenty-five millionth of an inch.

nematocyst Stinging structure in some cells of corals, sea anemones, and jellyfish.

neuron A nerve cell.

neurotransmitter Chemical that carries a nerve signal across a synapse.

nodes of Ranvier Tiny gaps in the myelin sheath across which nerve signals jump.

nuclear envelope Membrane surrounding the nucleus.

nucleus Organelle that contains a eukaryote cell's DNA.

oncogene Gene that causes cancer.

organelle Membrane-lined structures inside eukaryote cells, such as the nucleus.

paracrine signaling Short-distance signaling between cells.

peroxisome Organelle that breaks down toxins.

phloem Plant tissue that carries dissolved sugars.

photosynthesis The conversion of water and carbon dioxide into sugars in plants, using the energy of sunlight.

phragmoplast Structure on which cell walls form during cell division in plants.

plasmodesmatum Structure linking two plant cells that allows water and small molecules to move from one to the other.

prokaryote cell Cell of a bacterium, which does not contain organelles.

protein Molecule formed by amino acids in the ribosome.

proto-oncogene Gene that controls the timing of each stage of the cell cycle.

red blood cell Cell that carries oxygen and carbon dioxide around the body.

ribosome Granule on which protein production occurs.

rigor mortis Stiffness of the muscles after death.

rough endoplasmic reticulum Organelle on the surface of which ribosomes occur.

sarcomere Unit of muscle that contracts.

smooth endoplasmic reticulum Organelle that packages proteins ready for export from the cell and also produces some lipids.

sperm Male sex cell

spindle Cagelike structure that forms during cell division along which the chromosomes align and move.

stem cell Cell that has yet to differentiate (change) into a particular type of cell.

synapse Gap between the ends of two neurons.

transpiration Process of water loss at the leaves of a plant.

tumor A mass of cells started by a single cell that divides uncontrollably; can be benign or malignant (cancerous).

tumor-suppressor gene Gene that inhibits cell division.

turgor pressure Pressure exerted by water-filled cavities in plant cells that keeps plants erect.

xylem Plant tissue through which water is transported.

zygote An egg fertilized by a sperm that will develop into a new organism.

Set Index

Numbers in **bold** refer to volumes; page numbers in *italics* refer to picture captions.

A

adaptations **1**:12–13; **9**:23–25, 51
adaptive radiation **9**:49–50
ADHD **8**:61
aging **8**:62–70
alcohol **5**:51
algae **2**:9; **4**:6, 21, 22, 24, 28, 29; **5**:5; **8**:10
alleles **3**:6, 10, 11, 12–15, 42, 53, 54–55, 62; **8**:17; **9**:27, 33–34, 37, 38
allergies **3**:62
alternation of generations **5**:41–43, 69; **8**:36
amebas **2**:26–27; **3**:38; **4**:20, 22, 23, 25, 29
amino acids **1**:32–33; **7**:9
amniocentesis **3**:57
amphibians **6**:8, 23; **9**:58
anabolic reactions **1**:34, 35
antibiotics **2**:23; **4**:16, 54–55, 68–69; **9**:13
antibodies **1**:33–34; **4**:49; **7**:69, 70
ants **3**:44; **5**:22; **6**:46, 67
aphids **6**:46, 48, 68–69; **8**:15
appendix **1**:26–27
arteries **7**:23, 24
arthritis **8**:68
arthropods **1**:18
atmosphere **10**:22–23
atoms **1**:10, 11, 28
Australopithecus **6**:47; **9**:62, 63, 64–65
autopsies **1**:56
autotomy **6**:44, 45
auxin **5**:25, 26, 27, 29

B

bacteria **1**:7, 16; **4**:4, 8–19
  antibiotic-resistant **4**:16, 55, 60, 68–69; **9**:13
  artificial **1**:13
  cell walls **2**:23
  conjugation **8**:17
  and disease **4**:19, 44, 46, 48
  extreme lives **4**:6–7, 8, 11, 12
  flagella **2**:28
  in food production **4**:10, 11, 57–59
  and genetic engineering **3**:63–64, 65–66; **4**:60–63, 68
  genomes **3**:45–47
  grown on gel **1**:54
  light-producing **6**:59
  mining using **4**:69
  and plastics **1**:37; **4**:65
  and pollutants **4**:63–67
  recycling elements **4**:6, 9
  reproduction **1**:8; **4**:18–19; **8**:62–63
bacteriophages **4**:43, 62
balance **7**:57
bats **6**:14, 64; **9**:46
beach zones **5**:67
beer **4**:58
beetles **1**:70; **3**:64; **4**:61; **6**:17, 41, 46, 56
benzene **1**:28–29
bile **7**:14
binary fission **2**:53–54; **4**:18; **8**:9–10
biochemistry **1**:28–37
biodiversity **1**:23; **10**:9
biofeedback **7**:40–41
biological clocks **8**:41
biological control **1**:63; **6**:62
bioluminescence **4**:24

biomes **1**:11; **6**:32; **10**:8–9, 29–36
biosphere **1**:11; **10**:28–29
bird feeders **1**:42
birds **6**:8–9, 11, 12–13, 33, 39; **10**:37
  adaptive radiation **9**:49–50
  care for young **6**:56–57
  defense **6**:47
  eggs **2**:4; **6**:54
  evolution **9**:60; **10**:37
  flight **6**:25–26
  mutualism **6**:58–59
  reproduction **6**:50; **8**:27–28
blood **7**:23, 24–25, 28, 29–31
  cells **2**:10, 15, 59–60; **7**:25, 67, 68–69
  separation **1**:51
bones **2**:16; **7**:34–40
brain **2**:18; **7**:47–54, 57; **8**:58–59
  cancer **2**:67
breathing **7**:26–33
bryophytes **5**:5
budding **1**:8, 9; **8**:8
Burgess Shale **9**:57
butterflies **6**:29, 42; **8**:38, 39–40; **9**:60, 61

C

camouflage **6**:4, 19, 39; **9**:20
cancer **1**:51; **2**:56, 62–70; **3**:19, 58; **8**:67
capillaries **7**:23, 24
captive breeding **10**:68–69
carbohydrates **1**:30–31; **7**:9–10, 13
carbon **1**:29–30; **10**:12–14
carbon dioxide **7**:24, 28, 30; **10**:53
carnivores **6**:10, 12
catabolic reactions **1**:34–35
cats **1**:16, 17, 24–25; **3**:42; **9**:24–25

cells **1**:11; **2**:4–19; **3**:16–17; **8**:67
  communication **2**:44–51
  division **2**:24, 53–61; **3**:6–7, 17,
    18–25, 43–44
  internal structure **2**:30–43
  movement **2**:26–29
  support **2**:13, 20–26
cellulose **1**:31; **5**:8–9; **10**:12, 13
centrifuges **1**:51
CFCs **10**:23, 60
Chagas' disease **4**:29, 31
charts **1**:58, 59, 60, 61
cheetahs **6**:17, 24, 69
Chernobyl disaster **10**:57
childbirth **8**:47–50
childhood **8**:58–59
chimpanzees **3**:50; **6**:65
chitin **1**:36
chloroplasts **2**:12, 39–40; **5**:8
cholera **4**:47, 54, 67
chromatin **3**:17–18
chromatography **1**:52, 53, 54
chromosomes **2**:33, 58; **3**:5, 6,
    18–25, 39–40, 43–44, 50–53;
    8:9; **9**:28
  abnormalities **3**:57–58
  sex **3**:51–52, 55–56, 57–58
cilates **4**:22, 24, 25, 26
cilia and flagella **2**:27–29
circulatory system **7**:6–7, 18–24
cladistics **1**:18–19
classification **1**:14–20
climate **10**:18–27
clones **1**:64, 65; **3**:66–68; **5**:31,
    46, 47
cnidarians **2**:19
coelacanths **6**:8
cold, common **4**:39
color blindness **3**:55
colors **7**:59, 60

commensalisms **6**:60
communication **6**:66–70
communities **1**:11; **10**:7, 8
compost **4**:7
computing **1**:68–70
conifers **5**:21–22
conservation **9**:39, 41; **10**:62–69
continents, moving **9**:12–13
contraception **8**:50
coral reefs **10**:46–47
corals **4**:6, 29; **8**:40, 41
courtship **6**:51; **8**:27
cowbirds **6**:52
cows **10**:12
crabs **6**:39; **8**:35, 37
crayfish **6**:69
creationism **9**:7, 11
crocodiles **6**:8, 23, 54, 58–59
crops **4**:34, 62–63; **5**:44–56, 60
cyanobacteria **4**:12–13, 17; **9**:55
cystic fibrosis **1**:36

D
Darwin, Charles **5**:27–28, 38; **9**:4,
    6–7, 16, 17–21, 28, 62;
    10:37, 39
data analysis **1**:58–61
DDT **10**:60
death **2**:29; **7**:50
defense, animal **6**:38–47
deserts **5**:19–21; **6**:31–33;
    10:35–36
detergents, biological **1**:35
detrivores **6**:10, 13
diabetes **1**:31; **2**:44; **3**:65
diapause **6**:29
diaphragm **7**:32–33
diatoms **2**:53; **4**:5, 22, 23, 24, 26,
    27
diffusion **7**:27–28

digestive system **7**:7, 11–16
dimorphism, sexual **8**:28; **9**:67
dinoflagellates **4**:22, 23, 24, 27, 28,
    29, 30
dinosaurs **2**:16; **6**:9, 24; **9**:8, 58
disease **3**:56–57; **4**:19, 34, 39–40,
    44–55, 64; **7**:64, 65–66
dissection **1**:54–55, 56
diversity **6**:4–9; **9**:25
DNA **1**:7; **2**:33; **3**:4, 5, 27–29,
    38–39, 46; **9**:15, 28
  bacterial **2**:7; **4**:14–16, 60–61
  comparing **1**:27; **3**:43; **9**:62
  in computing **1**:68–70
  fingerprints **1**:55; **2**:6; **3**:6; **9**:31
  hybridization **1**:26
  junk **3**:39
  mitochondrial **2**:41; **3**:48–49;
    9:68
  protein formation **3**:31–36
  recombinant **3**:63; **4**:60
  replication **3**:18, 29–31, 32
  structure **1**:36, 37; **3**:26, 27, 36;
    9:29, 30
dodos **9**:53
dogs **1**:26; **3**:46; **6**:70
dolphins **6**:14, 70; **9**:59
domestication **3**:61
dominance **6**:67
drugs **4**:51, 54; **5**:49
  designer **1**:66–67
  recreational **5**:49–50

E
ears and hearing **6**:13; **7**:60–62
Earth **10**:29
echolocation **6**:14, 42–43
ecology **10**:4–9
ecosystems **1**:10–12; **10**:7, 28–39,
    30, 40–49

ecotourism **10**:61

eggs **2**:4; **6**:52–54; **8**:19, 24, 32–33, 34, 43; **9**:50

electric fields **6**:15, 67

electrophoresis **1**:53–54, 55

elements **1**:28, 29

elephants **1**:27; **6**:68

embryos **1**:24; **8**:54, 55

endocrine system **2**:48; **7**:54–55; **8**:59–60

endoplasmic reticulum **2**:33–35, 46

energy **2**:42; **10**:10–11, 61

enzymes **1**:33, 34–35; **3**:29; **4**:58–59

digestive **7**:11, 13–14

restriction **4**:60–61

epithelium **2**:14–15

ergonomics **1**:70

esophagus **7**:13

estivation **6**:31

estrus cycle **8**:23–24

euglenoids **4**:22, 25

eukaryotes **1**:14, 15–16; **2**:7, 8–9, 30–31, 53; **4**:9, 21–23; **9**:55–56

evolution **9**:4–15, 35–40, 44–53, 54–61

convergent **1**:20, 21; **9**:11–12, 14, 51–53, 59

eukaryote **2**:7

genetics and **9**:26–31

human **3**:59; **9**:62–70

on islands **10**:37

iterative **9**:52

rates **9**:10, 42

excretion **1**:7; **7**:8, 17

experiments **1**:39, 41, 56, 59–60

extinctions **9**:53, 57, 58; **10**:54, 69–70

eyes **7**:57–60; **9**:27

F

falcons, peregrine **10**:68–69

farming **1**:62–63; **3**:60, 61, 64; **5**:18, 45; **10**:50–51, 60

fats **1**:32; **7**:10, 14

feeding **1**:7; **6**:10–19

fermentation **4**:10, 57–58

fertilization **8**:19, 25–27

in vitro **2**:54

plant **5**:37–39, 40

self **8**:15

fertilizers **10**:15, 16, 48

fetuses **2**:18; **8**:55, 59

fiber **5**:54–55

field studies **1**:38–47, 58

finches, Galápagos **9**:17, 49–50; **10**:37

fires **5**:22

fish **6**:8, 15, 19, 36, 37, 59

deep-sea **10**:44–45

defense **6**:46–47

evolution **9**:57–58

flying **6**:38–39

fossil **9**:7

reproduction **6**:53; **8**:4, 16, 26

swimming **6**:22–23

fishing **10**:42

flagellates **4**:22, 29

Fleming, Alexander **4**:19

flies **1**:5, 70; **8**:37; **9**:28

flight **6**:25–27

flowers **1**:56; **5**:34, 37, 38, 43, 56, 57

food **2**:42; **5**:69; **7**:8–11, 24, 65

from microorganisms **4**:10, 56–59

genetically modified **3**:62, 66; **4**:60; **6**:22

food chains and webs **4**:6; **5**:6; **10**:4–5, 6, 41

foraminiferans **4**:22, 23, 25

forests **6**:33–35; **10**:8, 34–35

see also rainforests

fossils **1**:22; **4**:25; **9**:7, 8, 9–11, 42, 57

imprints **9**:56

looking for **9**:61

tracks **9**:66

founder effect **9**:38–39

foxes, fennec **6**:31

freshwater habitats **6**:37; **10**:48–49

frogs **6**:23–24; **8**:25

fruit, ripening **5**:29–30

fuels **4**:69–70; **10**:14

fungi **1**:21; **2**:9; **4**:44–45; **5**:5, 13

G

Gaia hypothesis **10**:65

Galen, Claudius **7**:5, 6–7

galls **6**:46

gas exchange **7**:24, 28–29

gender **3**:51; **8**:20–21, 29

gene flow **9**:37, 39–40

gene pools **1**:23; **9**:29, 36, 37

gene probes **3**:46

genera **1**:16, 17

genes **2**:33; **3**:4–5, 6, 7, 11, 27–29, 34, 38–39; **8**:16–18; **9**:20, 26, 28, 29, 32–33

compared **1**:26, 27

control of **2**:12, 66–67; **3**:36–37, 47; **8**:56–57

interaction **3**:40–41

linked **3**:14, 40, 55–56

mapping **3**:58–59

testing **3**:55

gene therapy **2**:68; **3**:68–70

genetic disorders **9**:31

genetic drift **9**:26, 36–37, 39

genetic engineering **3**:63–66;
    4:59–63, 68; **5**:30–31
genetic modificiation (GM) **1**:64;
    3:7; **4**:60, 62–63, 66–67; **5**:34
genetics **3**:4–7
    applied **3**:60–70
    human **3**:50–59; **9**:40
    population **9**:32–43
genomes **3**:5, 38–49, 50–52
genotypes **3**:11, 42–43, 54–55
gestation **6**:55
gliding **6**:25, 26
global warming **10**:24, 25, 53,
    58–59
glucose **1**:30, 31, 34, 35
glue, casein **1**:32
glycerol **1**:32
glycogen **1**:31; **7**:16
Golgi apparatus **2**:35
gorillas **6**:64, 65
grafting **5**:47
Gram stain **2**:23; **4**:15
graphs **1**:60–61
grasses **5**:18
grasslands **6**:35; **10**:33
greenhouse gases **10**:23–24, 58, 59
Green Revolution **1**:62
group living **6**:47, 62–65
growth **1**:9; **8**:57–61
guano **10**:16–17

H
habitats **1**:11; **6**:28–29, 32;
    10:5–6, 8
    loss **10**:51–53, 66
Haeckel, Ernst **1**:24
handedness **7**:52
healing **3**:18
heart **7**:18, 19–23
heart attacks **2**:46

heart disease **7**:24
height **9**:27
hemoglobin **1**:25, 33; **7**:24, 30, 31
hemophilia **3**:56
hepatitis **4**:42–43, 50
herbivores **6**:10–12, 13
herds **6**:47, 62–63; **9**:52
hermaphrodites **6**:49; **8**:20–21
hibernation **6**:28–29; **9**:24
HIV/AIDS **4**:33, 37–38, 40, 41,
    46–47, 50, 55; **7**:70; **8**:53
homeostasis **7**:7
honeybees **6**:70
hoof-and-mouth disease **4**:46
Hooke, Robert **2**:5
hormones **1**:33; **2**:48–49; **7**:10,
    54–55; **8**:22–23, 47,
    59–60, 69
    plant **5**:24–31
horses, evolution **9**:10, 11
HRT **8**:69
human development **8**:54–61
Human Genome Project **3**:7, 15,
    45, 58–59
humors **1**:4
hunting **6**:17–19
Huxley, Thomas **9**:7
hybrids **1**:17; **3**:62–63; **9**:45
hydras **8**:8
hydrothermal vents **10**:45
hypothalamus **7**:50, 55; **8**:60
hypotheses **1**:39, 59, 61

I
immune system **4**:49; **7**:25, 64,
    66–70
immunization and vaccines **1**:66;
    4:40, 42, 49–51, 67; **7**:64, 65,
    67, 68
imprinting **6**:57

inbreeding **9**:40–42
infertility **8**:50–51, 52
inflammatory response **7**:66,
    67, 68
inheritance **3**:8–15
insects **1**:70; **6**:6, 14, 37
    eggs **6**:52–53
    exoskeleton **1**:36; **7**:36
    flight **6**:25, 26
    growth **8**:38–39
    mimicry by **6**:40
    nighttime **1**:44
    social **6**:63
insulin **1**:31, 33; **2**:48; **3**:40, 65–66;
    4:68; **8**:65
intestines **7**:14–15
introns and exons **3**:34
invertebrates **6**:6–7; **8**:12–13, 23
islands **9**:38; **10**:37–38

J
jellyfish **6**:6, 16, 22; **8**:36
Jenner, Edward **1**:66; **4**:50
joints **7**:34–35, 39–40

K
kangaroos **6**:24, 55
karyotypes **3**:22, 39–40
Kekulé, Friedrich A. **1**:28–29
kidneys **7**:17
Koch, Robert **1**:54; **4**:5, 47, 55

L
laboratory methods **1**:48–57
Lamarckism **9**:5–6, 16
language, human **6**:70
larvae **8**:36, 37, 38
learning **7**:53
leaves **2**:12–13; **5**:10, 11–12, 26, 29
Leeuwenhoek, Anton van **4**:5, 50

lichens **8**:11
life **1**:4–13, 10, 30; **9**:54–61
life cycles **8**:10, 30–41
life expectancy **7**:64–65; **8**:63–67
ligaments **7**:40
Linnaeus, Carolus **1**:14, 16
lipids **1**:32, 36
Lister, Joseph **4**:52
liver **7**:16
lizards **6**:20, 22, 33, 44; **8**:14
Lorenzo's oil **2**:43
"Lucy" skeleton **9**:65
lungs **2**:62; **7**:28–29, 31–32, 33,
    65; **8**:68
lymphatic system **7**:68, 69–70
lymphocytes **7**:69, 70
lysosomes **2**:37–38

M
malaria **4**:30, 31, 45, 52, 53, 54
mammals **1**:24; **6**:9, 55–56;
    9:60–61
  forelimbs **1**:25, 26
  reproduction **1**:8; **6**:55; **8**:28–29
mantises **6**:51, 52
Mars **1**:13; **4**:70
marsupials **9**:12–13, 51, 52
mating **6**:51–52; **8**:27–29
measles **4**:40, 41
medicine **1**:65–67
meiosis **2**:60–61; **3**:7, 21–25,
    43–44, 52–53; **9**:28, 34
memory **7**:53–54
Mendel, Gregor **3**:8–15, 26;
    9:20–21, 28
menopause **8**:69–70
menstrual cycle **8**:23–24, 45
metabolism **1**:35
metamorphosis **8**:38–39
metazoans **9**:56–57

meteorites, from Mars **1**:13
mice **9**:23
microorganisms **1**:9; **4**:4–7, 44–55,
    56–70
  in the gut **4**:6; **6**:12, 59
microscopes **1**:6, 49–51; **2**:5
migrations **6**:29
milk **6**:55–56
mimicry **6**:39–40, 41–42, 43, 46
mind, theory of **6**:65
minerals **7**:10–11; **10**:17
miscarriage **8**:50–51
mites **6**:25, 60
mitochondria **2**:7, 41–42
mitosis **2**:56–58; **3**:7, 18–20
moas **9**:25
molecules **1**:10, 11, 28
monkeys **6**:68, 69; **9**:23
monosaccharides **1**:30, 31; **7**:9
mosquitoes **4**:30, 45, 52, 53;
    6:61–62
mosses **8**:10, 12
moths **6**:39, 42–43, 68
mountains **6**:30; **10**:20–21, 32–33
movement **1**:7–8; **4**:17–18;
    6:20–27
multiple fission **8**:10
multiple sclerosis **2**:51
muscles **2**:16–17, 20, 29; **6**:20;
    7:40–43
  cardiac **7**:18–19, 42
mushrooms **3**:48; **8**:10
mutations **2**:63–67; **4**:55; **9**:21–22,
    29–31, 35, 43
mutualism **4**:6; **6**:58, 70

N
nails **2**:52
names, scientific **1**:16; **9**:44
neo-Darwinism **9**:22

nerves **7**:45, 48
nervous system **7**:27, 44–54, 55
neurons (nerve cells) **2**:17–18, 51,
    61; **7**:44, 45, 46, 48
newts **6**:41
niches **10**:6–7
nitrogen **4**:6, 9; **5**:17; **10**:14–16, 22
nocturnal animals **6**:15
nose **7**:63, 67
nucleic acids **1**:35–37
  see also DNA; RNA
nucleotides **1**:27, 36; **3**:27
nucleus **2**:32–33

O
oceans **6**:35–37, 49; **10**:41–48, 58
oil spills **4**:64; **10**:59
omnivores **6**:10, 11
organelles **1**:16; **2**:8–9, 30, 33–43;
    3:17
organization, biological **1**:10–13
organs **1**:10, 11; **2**:6; **7**:5
osmosis **4**:28
osteoporosis **7**:38; **8**:68, 69
oxygen **5**:10; **7**:23–24, 27–28,
    30–31; **10**:22
ozone layer **9**:55; **10**:23

P
pacemakers, heart **1**:65–66
pain **7**:46
painkillers **2**:48
pancreas **2**:48
pandas **6**:11; **10**:70
pandemics **4**:46
parasites **4**:29; **5**:19; **6**:12, 60–62;
    8:33; **9**:61
parental care **8**:33–36
Parkinson's disease **2**:50
parthenogenesis **8**:13–14, 15, 18

Pasteur, Louis **4**:5, 47, 50, 67
peacocks **8**:28; **9**:18
pedomorphosis **8**:38
penicillin **4**:19
peristalsis **7**:13
peroxisomes **2**:38–39
pest control **1**:63; **3**:64; **4**:38, 61, 63; **6**:62
pesticides **10**:60, 68
phagocytes **4**:48; **7**:66, 68–69, 70
phenotype **3**:11
pheromones **6**:68, 69
phloem **2**:14; **5**:10–11
phosphorus **10**:16–17
photosynthesis **4**:13, 24; **5**:4, 7, 10; **10**:10
Piltdown Man **9**:64
pituitary gland **7**:49, 54, 55; **8**:60
plankton **4**:27, 28; **6**:30; **8**:36–37; **10**:41, 42
plants **1**:6, 22; **5**:1–23
  cells **2**:8, 9, 11–14, 22–23, 38, 46, 59; **3**:20; **5**:4–5, 6–9
  cloned **3**:66–67; **5**:31
  counting **1**:46
  hormones **5**:24–31
  parasites **5**:19
  and people **5**:44–57
  reproduction and propagation **5**:32–43; **8**:10–12, 22
  sensitivity **1**:9
  viruses **4**:38–39
  water plants **10**:12
plasmids **3**:63–64; **4**:16, 55, 60–61
plastics, biodegradable **1**:37; **4**:65
plovers **6**:54, 58–59
pneumonia **4**:37
polar regions **6**:28, 29–31, 36; **10**:30–31, 58–59
polio **4**:34, 37, 39–40, 50

pollen and pollination **5**:34, 35–37, 40; **8**:10, 18
pollution **4**:63–67; **5**:12; **6**:36; **7**:30; **10**:36, 56–61
polymerase chain reaction **3**:37
polypeptides **1**:33
polyploids **3**:25, 38, 44, 61; **9**:47–48
ponds **6**:37; **10**:49
populations **1**:11; **10**:7, 38–39
  genetics **9**:32–43
Portuguese man-o'-war **6**:63
predators **6**:12–13, 14–16, 17; **10**:38–39
pregnancy **8**:45–48
primates **6**:64–65; **9**:62
prions **4**:42
prokaryotes **1**:14, 16; **2**:7, 30, 52, 53–54; **4**:9; **9**:55
prostheses **7**:41
proteins **1**:10, 32–34, 36; **3**:5, 29, 31–36; **7**:9
protists **2**:9; **4**:4–6, 20–31; **8**:9, 17
protozoa **4**:21
puberty **8**:61
punctuated equilibria **9**:42–43
Punnett squares **3**:10

Q
quadrats **1**:40

R
rabies **4**:50
radiolarians **4**:22, 23, 25, 28–29
rain, acid **10**:58
rainforests **1**:46; **6**:34–35; **10**:34–35, 53
recombination **9**:33–34
red tides **4**:30
reflexes **7**:47

remora fish **6**:60
reproduction **1**:9; **6**:48–57; **8**:4–7, 42–53
  asexual **1**:8; **4**:18, 27; **5**:32–33, 35; **6**:48; **8**:5, 8–15
  sexual **1**:8; **4**:26; **5**:33–35; **6**:48, 49–50; **8**:4–5, 16–29; **9**:51
reptiles **6**:8, 23; **9**:50, 58–60
reserves, ecological **10**:66–67
respiration **1**:7, 34–35; **7**:31; **10**:14
respiratory system **7**:28–29
ribosomes **2**:34
RNA **1**:7, 36, 37; **2**:33; **3**:31, 32–36, 58
robots **7**:55
root nodules **10**:16
roots **5**:13, 20, 24, 29
roundworms **8**:65
rubber **5**:55
ruminants **9**:50–51

S
saliva **7**:12, 13
sampling **1**:42–45
sandgrouse **6**:33
sargassum **5**:63
scavengers **6**:12
SCID **3**:69–70
scorpions **6**:15, 51; **8**:23
scrublands **10**:35–36
sea cucumbers **6**:45
sea hares **6**:45
seahorses **6**:53; **8**:26
sea levels **10**:24
seals **1**:12, 13, 26
sea mice **1**:68
seashores **10**:46, 47–48
seasons **10**:20–21
sea urchins **8**:65
seawater **10**:40

seaweeds **5**:5, 58–70

seeds **1**:8, 9; **5**:39–40, 41, 46; **8**:5

selection

    artificial **9**:6, 21

    natural **9**:4–5, 6, 16–25, 35, 36

    sexual **9**:18

selective breeding **1**:63–64; **3**:60–63; **8**:6, 7

senses **1**:9; **6**:13–15; **7**:56–63

sensitivity **1**:9

sewage treatment **4**:13, 66, 67

sharks **6**:19, 35

sheep **3**:67–68; **9**:6, 52

shells **6**:44–45

silicon, life based on **1**:30

skeletons **1**:36; **7**:34–35, 36, 38–39

    hydrostatic **6**:20–22

skin **2**:31, 65; **7**:67

sleeping sickness **4**:29, 30–31

slugs **6**:23, 49

smallpox **1**:66; **4**:40, 41, 45–46, 50, 51, 67

smell, sense of **6**:14; **7**:62–63

smoking **5**:51; **7**:32, 65

snails **1**:44; **6**:16–17, 21, 23, 44–45

snakes **6**:8, 14–15, 16, 43, 54

    hind limbs **1**:26, 27; **9**:15

social groups **8**:28–29

soil **10**:27

sound **6**:43, 68

species **1**:14–15, 17, 20–25, 45; **9**:45–46

    cryptic **9**:46

    genetic markers **1**:27

    indicator **10**:10

    introduced **5**:56; **10**:55

    new **9**:38, 39, 42–43, 45, 46–48

    plant **5**:33

    rainforest **1**:46

sperm **2**:11; **8**:19, 24–25, 27, 42, 44

spiders **6**:16, 19, 21, 47, 68

    reproduction **6**:51–52, 53; **8**:27

spinal cord **7**:45, 46

sponges **2**:18–19; **8**:13

spontaneous generation **1**:5; **4**:47; **9**:5

spores **5**:32–33; **8**:10, 11–12

sporozoans **4**:22

squid **6**:22, 45, 59

starch **1**:31

STDs **8**:51–53

stem cells **2**:18, 60; **8**:56

stems **2**:13; **5**:12–13, 16

steroids **1**:32; **7**:43

stomach **7**:7, 13–14

stromatolites **1**:22

sugar **2**:48; **5**:48

surveys **1**:43

symbiosis **4**:6, 28–29; **6**:58–62

symmetry **6**:4–5

systems, body **1**:10, 11; **7**:4–7

T

tails **9**:12

tapeworms **6**:5, 12, 60, 61

Tasmanian wolves **10**:54

taste **7**:13, 62, 63

teeth **7**:12

tendons **7**:42

thalamus **7**:49

tigers **6**:66–67

time, geological **9**:55

tissues **1**:10, 11; **7**:4–5

toads **6**:18, 46–47, 53; **10**:55

tongue **7**:13, 63

tortoises, giant **3**:49; **9**:17–18

touch **7**:56–57

tracking **1**:45–47

transpiration **5**:8, 9

transplants **7**:18, 23, 49

traps **1**:40, 41, 44

tree rings **10**:25

trees **5**:12–13, 15, 27, 52–53; **8**:30

trophic levels **10**:11

tropisms **5**:28–29

trypanosomes **4**:29, 30–31

tuberculosis **4**:52–53

tundras **6**:30; **10**:31–32

turtles **8**:21; **10**:52, 69

twins **3**:53–54; **8**:46–47; **9**:34

V

vacuoles **2**:35–37, 38

variation **3**:22, 41; **9**:21–22, 27

veins **7**:23, 24

ventilators **7**:32

vertebrates **6**:7–9; **9**:57–58

vestigial features **1**:26–27; **9**:12, 15

viroids **4**:34

viruses **1**:7; **3**:35, 64; **4**:6–7, 32–43, 34, 44, 55

    and cancer **2**:64

    computer **4**:43

vitamins **7**:10

W

wasps, parasitic **1**:63; **6**:47, 62

water **10**:26–27

weeds **8**:12, 31–32; **9**:25

wetlands **10**:49, 52

whales **6**:17, 23, 56; **9**:15, 42; **10**:43

whaling **10**:54, 65, 67

wood **5**:52–53

worms **6**:5, 12, 21, 49

X, Y

xylem **2**:13–14; **5**:9–10

yeast **1**:10; **4**:56–57, 58